To the _____

Keep training hard!

Mortal Doctor

A Story of Transformation, Discipline and Purpose.

By Phillip Ahn, M.D.

Phillip Ahn, MD
"Shin Tony" MKII

Table of Contents

Acknowledgements	3
Foreword	4
Introduction	6
Chapter 1: Made in Korea	10
Chapter 2: Coming to America	16
Chapter 3: Becoming An American	29
Chapter 4: Inheriting Values	42
Chapter 5: School of Hard Knocks	45
Chapter 6: Self-esteem	51
Chapter 7: Heaven on Earth	56
Chapter 8: Study Lessons	61
Chapter 9: Pranks and Prayer	71
Chapter 10: College: Purgatory	75
Chapter 11: Global Perspective	85
Chapter 12: Gap Year	90
Chapter 13: Hittin' the Books	96
Chapter 14: Adversity in Africa	101
Chapter 15: Rockford Files	110
Chapter 16: Taking the Hippocratic Oath	119

Chapter 17: Residencia Médica	**127**
Chapter 18: Mortal Kombat 2	**135**
Chapter 19: Moral Kombat	**148**
Chapter 20: Fame Without Fortune	**154**
Chapter 21: Ahn's Academy of Taekwondo	**166**
Chapter 22: Práctica Médica	**172**
Chapter 23: Life Goes On	**183**
Chapter 24: Parenthood	**189**
Chapter 25: Lifelong Athlete	**200**
Chapter 26: Marital Kombat	**206**
Chapter 27: Mercy Tragedy	**213**
Chapter 28: Fame Resurrected	**216**
Chapter 29: Dance Fever	**226**
Author's Note	**233**
Favorite Quotes	**234**
Favorite Jokes	**237**
Appendix	**244**

Acknowledgements

To my family, friends, fellow Mortal Kombat 2 characters and all my fans: you have all significantly contributed to my incredibly abundant and joyful life. Thank you.

To Doc Mack, Jim Mack, Jeff Lee and Steve Koran: thank you for your support and edits.

To my editor Shelly Hanson: your incredible insights and creative ideas have made this book possible.

To my daughter Abygale: you are the inspiration for everything I do. I love you.

Foreword

by Doc Mack, Owner of Galloping Ghost Arcade

From Phillip Ahn's video game persona, Shang Tsung, a sorcerer who hosts tournaments where kombatants fight to the death, you would have no idea what to expect when meeting him in person.

To many video game players, Phillip had great notoriety from having his name in the credits of the Mortal Kombat II arcade game. While many of us knew his name, we did not know the man behind the character. For me, I remember walking into a local arcade shortly after Mortal Kombat II was released, and the counter had an advertisement offering autographed photos of the legendary fighter.

For the decade I've known Phillip, he has always been a fairly guarded person, letting his achievements speak for themselves. Talking with Phillip as he worked on his book has given a greater insight to the foundation of the path he has forged in life. His diverse interests have garnered him many titles: martial artist, video game icon, doctor, father, dancer, teacher, traveler and now author.

Looking back at the original autographed photo, the words of wisdom Phillip wrote to me still hold true. In this memoir, he shares his knowledge and experiences from his journey through life with everyone. For readers following a similar path, it may grant motivation to continue forward. For those struggling to find a path, it may give the inspiration needed to start forging one of their own. For everyone else, it is sure to entertain.

Introduction

The initials, "M.D." stands for "Medical Doctor." In the case of Dr. Phillip Ahn, these letters can also stand for many other aspects of his life: Multi-Dimensional, Motivator and Disciplinarian, Mentor and Disciple, Multilingual Diversity, Missionary to Developing countries, Music and Dance, Marriage and Divorce, Mindful Dad, Marvelous Daughter, and possibly more not mentioned above. Dr. Ahn would like people to consider him as "a jack of many trades and a master of a few."

Dr. Ahn is a board certified family physician who has served the needy in the south side of Chicago for his entire medical career. He has also made over 25 medical mission trips to developing countries in Latin America, Africa, and the Caribbean. However, he is most famous for his portrayal of the character "Shang Tsung" in the very popular video game, "Mortal Kombat 2" (MK 2).

This game has been played by male and female gamers, including the young and the not so young. Mortal Kombat 2 has maintained popularity in all areas of the world, for over 25 years, since he filmed his role and helped launch it in 1993. Phillip's continual involvement with the Mortal Kombat community has earned him fans across every continent.

Phillip Ahn was not always in the limelight. Ironically, there was a previous actor named Philip Ahn, who passed away before this Phillip Ahn helped popularize Mortal Kombat 2. (Note the difference in spelling.) To distinguish himself from the aforementioned actor, Dr. Ahn used his full name and his degree, Phillip Ahn, M.D., in his credits. One can see this at the end of the game if the player is able to defeat the game.

This book is about how a normal but very shy immigrant kid overcame his insecurities, low self-esteem and lack of self-discipline to develop into a very successful physician and martial artist. It also describes his cultivation of other talents and disciplines, all while serving the needy in Chicago and developing countries.

Dr. Ahn decided to write a memoir to better connect with his fans, friends and family so that they can better understand this normally reserved and private man. His hope is that by reading this book, people of all ages can be inspired to become the best that they can be. Phillip's goal is that his readers will "not just survive, but thrive" in life. He will accomplish this through sharing intimate moments of his past, as well as the life lessons and practical advice that he provides throughout the book. He desires that his readers will transform ("morph") and overcome whatever obstacles they perceive to be their shortcomings. After reading his book, Phillip wants readers to proceed to lead productive lives, demonstrating that they can make the most of their God-given talents and opportunities.

    Phillip was going to write his autobiography in the third person because he did not want to sound like he was bragging or boasting about his accomplishments. After consulting his trusted friends and family, he decided to heed their advice and write in the first person. He made this decision to help the readers to relate more to him as a normal person and to better experience the life circumstances that he has both endured and enjoyed. Humor is an important narrative tool ; by entertaining with true moments of laughter, Phillip hopes to better connect with his readers. He does not, by any means, want to offend anyone through his comments or jokes. Phillip hopes to connect with his friends and fans from all walks of life for which he is extremely grateful.

Chapter 1: Made in Korea

I was born in Seoul, South Korea and my birth name was "Ahn Soon Kyu". In Korea you are called by your last name first,

---

[1] Me (6 y.o.) and my brother (4 y.o.) at our dad's TKD school, Seoul.

followed by your first and middle names. Also in Korea, you are considered one year old when you are born and then turn two years old on January 1 of the following calendar year. So, if you are born on December 31, like my brother-in-law was, you are considered two years old the next day, when in reality you are one *day* old!

I am the oldest of four; I have one brother and two sisters. There are five years separating all four of us, so our parents were *very* busy when we were kids. My mom has told me that I was a very responsible child and a great caretaker, even wiping my siblings' behinds.

We grew up in a very small and crowded house, where my parents, paternal grandparents, aunts and uncles also lived. There were countless similar houses in our neighborhood. When I see cities in Colombia or Brazil, they remind me of my house in Seoul. My parents received college degrees from good universities, and they worked for the government in some capacity. My father also taught taekwondo part time. My dad was a strict disciplinarian, as the oldest of eight children, and his younger siblings revered him as a father figure or mentor. My mom was a micromanager of the household, as well as the "peacemaker" who caringly softened the blows of my father's punishment when we misbehaved.

I don't remember much about my life in Korea, but I remember that it was a developing country and that we struggled to live comfortably. Korea was under Japanese rule until the end of World War II. The Korean War soon followed, ending in 1953, at which time Korea was divided into North (Communist) and South (Democratic). South Korea transitioned to military rule after 1961, through General Park Chung Hee, who subsequently became president and remained so until his assassination in 1979. Park was the president when I lived in Korea. Even though he was, in essence, a dictator, he started the growth of a self-reliant economy and the modernization of South Korea. However, most of this growth happened after my family left Korea for the United States.

A vivid memory of Korea that I have is going to public baths with my mom and all of my siblings. We swam in our birthday suits in the big tubs while my mom bathed or socialized with her friends. I also remember eating some "street food" that I really enjoyed, like butterfly cocoons and squid jerky. One day when I was walking around my neighborhood, I saw smoke so I went to check it out. Some sanitation workers, "garbage men," were grilling a roadkill animal for a snack. It was a dead dog!

Corporal punishment was normal, even at school. If we did not turn in our homework, we had to stick out our palms and receive lashings with a stick from our teacher. If the stick broke on your hand while you were receiving your punishment, you had to bring a stick from your home the next day. One school day this happened to me, so I looked around my house and brought a soft and flimsy stick made of balsa wood that broke right away when the teacher swung it in the air. Everybody, including the teacher, laughed and I became very popular.

Speaking of popularity, there was a strange custom in Korea (at least at my school) involving kids in the same grade but in adjacent rooms. We physically fought each other before classes started, every morning! Maybe this is Korea's version of "turf wars" or "Mortal Kombat!" I became the designated leader and "pugilist." I am happy to say that I consistently defeated my "enemies." Maybe this was the first sign of the role that would be thrust upon me two decades later?

I briefly learned taekwondo from my father when I was six years old, taking lessons for six months. At that time, my father received his travel visa and immigrated to Chicago, Illinois, ahead of my mother and us children. The rest of the family followed and arrived in Chicago two years later, when I was eight years old.

I did not know anything about the United States of America when I grew up in Korea. Because Korea was a developing country at that time, many people dreamed of immigrating to America, known as "the Land of Opportunity." My parents knew they wanted a more comfortable life for themselves. More importantly, they wanted to provide their children the best possible opportunity to live "the American Dream." They wanted us to have the chance to become whatever we dreamed of becoming, without poverty or lack of resources as obstacles for our future.

    LIFE LESSON: Sometimes one must make great sacrifices and take big chances to chase your dreams, either for yourself or for your family.

Chapter 2: Coming to America

A couple of things about my trip from Korea to Chicago will forever be etched in my brain. First, my mom scolded me because I nearly caused my family to miss our flight by running around at the airport. We flew on Trans World Airlines, "TWA," which no longer exists. Second, I vividly remember looking out the window

---

[2] My siblings and me, soon after arriving in the United States.

of the plane and thinking that the clouds were icebergs. I did not realize that the plane flew above the clouds!

After three brief stops in Tokyo, Japan (I remember that there were a lot of electronics and toys there), Honolulu, Hawaii (I think I received a lei around my neck like in the movies) and Los Angeles (I do not remember anything about LA, not even the Hollywood sign since I couldn't read English), my family finally landed in Chicago. We were reunited with our father, and we arrived at our home, an apartment, in our dad's Buick LeSabre, to sleep in bunk beds. When I saw my father after two years, it seemed surreal. Our jet-lag clouded any memories of that first day together but we will forever be grateful for the sacrifices of our parents to be able to bring us to the United States.

We did not own a car or beds in Korea; we slept on blankets on the ground. Everything felt like a dream or a fantasy. The day we arrived in Chicago also happened to be October 31, Halloween. Why were Americans dressed in strange costumes?

Why were houses decorated with ghosts and goblins? What a first impression of America!

Soon after we arrived in the United States, our father took my brother and me to see "Enter The Dragon," starring Bruce Lee. I am sure that my dad, since he did not understand English, did not realize that this movie was rated "R" and contained inappropriate scenes for his young sons. I enjoyed the movie anyway and it is still one of my favorite movies. This movie was also a foreshadowing of things to come two decades later, when I would be invited to be a character in a video game that portrays a martial arts tournament similar to this movie.

Bruce Lee died just before our family immigrated to the United States. Elvis Presley died shortly after we immigrated to Chicago. I remember that my mom cried when she heard the news. Both of these people were famous throughout the world. For younger readers, Bruce Lee is considered the first martial artist to influence Western Civilization through his movies, instruction and philosophy. He invented his own martial art, Jeet Kune Do, after studying several martial arts. Elvis was also a pioneer, taking Blues music and combining it with Rock and Roll. "Elvis the Pelvis" even incorporated his martial arts techniques into his dance moves when he sang. He and The Beatles are often considered the most popular musicians in history.

*****

There were a variety of adjustments to living in the United States. In Korea, I lived in a small house and my whole family slept in one bedroom, while in the rest of this small house lived my grandparents, an aunt and three uncles. It was certainly smaller than I remembered it to be when I revisited it as an adult. An indoor bathroom was a luxury, one that our family could not afford. We all used an outhouse in Korea and the kids bathed with a hose outside in the yard. Waking us up on Saturday mornings, city workers would take away the "human waste" that we created in the outhouse.

I was shocked when a grade school friend threw away a half-eaten apple. When I left South Korea, it was a relatively poor country compared to the United States. My parents worked hard to provide food for our family and it was never wasted. If the entire extended family had fish for dinner one night, then we ate fish stew the next day, with left over bones and gills. I remember that I loved eating the eyes of the fish, as well as the eggs. (I don't understand why caviar is so expensive!) A banana was a treat, and I remember getting *one* banana for each of my birthdays.

Other examples of culture shock in America included eating with my hands, my first experience using no utensils, at a Pakistani friend's house. Oddly, I remember thinking that burgers were dirty if served by African Americans because I had never seen or interacted with anyone but Koreans prior to coming to America. Very quickly, this impression was erased, when I became friends with people of all races. When our father took the family to McDonald's for the first time, we, the kids, did not like the food.

Nevertheless, we quickly developed a liking for burgers and fries, like all Americans.

My mother took us to free medical and dental clinics because we were not rich. We took two buses (or a train and a bus) to get to these places because we had one car, that my father needed for his job. He initially worked at a factory before he started teaching taekwondo at YMCAs in Chicago and the suburbs. He eventually opened his own taekwondo school in northwest Chicago. My mother worked at a bank and I remember sleeping every night holding the Harris Bank lion. When I was around 12 years old, she left banking to open "In the Running," an athletic shoe store, attached to our taekwondo school.

Like typical Americans, my family also watched television. We did not have a TV in Korea. My brother and I started watching baseball and figured out, without understanding English, that Chicago had two teams. Naturally, we thought that these two teams played each other every day. My brother started cheering for the Cubs and I picked the White Sox.

We found some uniforms to be strange because they were multicolored, for example when the Sox played the Oakland A's or the Cubs played the Houston Astros. Back then, there was no inter-league play. The National League and American League teams never played each other, including the Cubs and Sox, except in the World Series. It was not until after a year of watching baseball that a friend enlightened us of this fact. Nevertheless, our allegiances stuck, and I have remained a loyal White Sox fan. Decades later, my daughter became a loyal Sox fan as well.

Besides baseball, the first TV shows that I remember watching in America were:

- Speed Racer
- Scooby Doo
- Tom and Jerry
- Popeye
- Woody Woodpecker
- Underdog
- the Pink Panther
- Spiderman
- Super Friends
- Hong Kong Phooey
- Looney Toons
- the Flintstones

- the Jetsons
- the Little Rascals
- the Ray Rayner Show
- Bozo's Circus
- the Brady Bunch
- Happy Days
- Welcome Back Kotter
- Starsky and Hutch
- Wonder Woman
- the Incredible Hulk
- the Six Million Dollar Man
- Baretta
- the Monkees

My dad liked the Three Stooges and the Lawrence Welk Show, but the kids found the latter boring. I guess we watched too much TV! I do not think we learned English through these shows. We did learn some English by watching Sesame Street, Electric Company (where Morgan Freeman got his start) and Zoom. Certain shows still spark enjoyment in my life, as I have sported a Flinstones or Looney Tunes (Bugs Bunny) tie to my clinic every Halloween!

*****

Even though I was a good student and a leader in elementary school in Korea, I became shy and insecure after I immigrated to Chicago, because I spoke no English. And, even though I did not understand English, I instinctively knew when other kids were making fun of me for being different, Asian. This led to several childhood skirmishes.

These incidents, where other kids made fun of me or my siblings, significantly decreased after a memorable incident in which I made one of the bullies cry in front of the other kids, including the bully's friends. I accomplished this feat by executing a perfect flying side kick, that knocked this bully down. The scene was like watching a movie. Seeing "Enter the Dragon" had already paid off!

I remember that there was one particular "big bully" in one of my classes. He picked on smaller kids, including myself. Decades after elementary school, while I was completing my family practice residency, a patient came into an occupational health clinic complaining of groin pain. Even though this patient was now an adult, I recognized him as being that bully in grade school. I confirmed this when I asked the patient if he went to the same grade school that I had attended on the north side of Chicago.

When this fact was confirmed, I told this patient that I was bullied by him in fourth grade. Caught with his pants down, the patient trembled when he stated, "That was a long time ago!" I reassured the patient and told him to relax. I treated him like any other patient and sent him on his way. This is one of the instances in which I found myself being "on the other side of the fence." I'm not a vengeful person and throughout my life I have learned to forgive and (usually) forget.

Bullying is a big problem that is pervasive, and with the rise of social media, social bullying has become common. The unfortunate and tragic consequences can lead to lifelong suffering and suicide by the victim, or even mass school shootings. I generally suffered childhood bullying in terms of racial bias and taunting. Through God's help and supportive friends, I was able to overcome my insecurities and to embrace my heritage and even thrive as an Asian American. I plead for my readers to take the time to find ways to connect with those you feel are different and reach out to hurting victims.

This moment with my childhood bully is an example of the fact that throughout my upbringing and into adulthood, I have maintained a great memory of people from my past. Some people have been more memorable than others, of course. I have run into people from my childhood and adolescence as an adult, and they have had no idea who I was because I was a very shy, inconspicuous child.

*****

My parents thought that it would be a good idea to start school in Chicago at a grade lower than kids my age, because of the language barrier. After one year, my academic progress was so good that my teachers, with my parents' blessing, "double promoted" me back to my normal grade. Unfortunately, this made schoolwork very hard for me and it led me to become even more shy and insecure. English is a very difficult language and it took me years to become comfortable speaking and writing it.

A year after immigrating to Chicago, my siblings and I decided not to speak Korean to each other to improve our English. We have almost always spoken English to each other since our pact. We still speak Korean to our parents, uncles and aunts.

I had a natural gift for mathematics. I scored high on standardized tests and obtained mostly A's in math classes. This allowed me to be accepted into Lane Tech High School, a great "magnet school" located on the northside of Chicago. I realize that there is a stereotype that Asians are gifted in math, but there is a bigger stereotype that all Asians work and study hard. I did *not* live up to this second stereotype until I entered college and learned to develop the proper study skills.

LIFE LESSON: Changing environments, especially moving to a culture with a language and traditions different than one's own, can be very difficult for people, especially children. Maladaptation to such changes can lead to children joining gangs, using drugs or succumbing to depression. I plead for my readers to welcome "new kids on the block" into their strange and intimidating surroundings by befriending and trying to understand them.

Chapter 3: Becoming An American

Our family lived in apartments in two racially diverse neighborhoods. My parents bought our first house on the northwest side of Chicago, before I entered seventh grade. We were the

---

[3] My best friend in junior high, Steve, and me at 8th grade graduation.

second non-Caucasian family to move into the neighborhood; the first was a Filipino family that had lived there for several years.

I am eternally grateful to Steve, who welcomed me into the neighborhood, befriended me, and became my best friend during my junior high school years. Steve, a quiet and hardworking blonde kid, helped this Korean transition into the traditionally all white neighborhood by including me in sports, activities at school and around the neighborhood. We played sports together, especially a modified baseball game called "fast pitch", in which the pitcher throws a rubber ball against the wall. In high school, the two of us challenged two other baseball teammates in this game. To their surprise, we stomped them by a score of 20-5. Steve has remained a good friend throughout the years and we still get together whenever he is in town or when I visit him.

My brother and I joined Little League baseball the summer before I entered seventh grade. Because we were shy and the only kids of color on our teams (like Ichiro Suzuki joining the Seattle Mariners in 2001), we did not give our names to teammates.

I had not yet started using an American name; officially, my name was still "Soon Ahn." Having to say my Korean name to kids with "normal" names was difficult for me. Our Little League teammates gave me the nickname "Spike" because I wore brand new, blue baseball spikes from my parents' sporting goods store. My brother received the nickname "Half Pint" because he was very small. I started going by "Phillip" when I entered high school and used it as my official first name when I became a naturalized American citizen in college.

My seventh grade teacher thought that my last name was "Soon," so she called me "Mr. Soon" until I finally corrected her at the end of the year! She also wrote in my eighth grade yearbook, "Good luck in high school. You will need it!" How can a teacher write that? In spite of this, because I knew she was a disciplinarian, like my dad and even myself later in life, I visited her regularly after graduation. To this day, I really respect teachers who approach their careers as "a calling."

During my junior high years, I would acquire other nicknames like "Bruce" (Lee, of course). One time when I was working at my dad's taekwondo school, a couple of kids came in. One of them looked at me, then at the poster of Bruce Lee on the wall, and then said to his friend, "Look, that's him!" I never met Bruce, or his son Brandon, but I did have the opportunity to meet his daughter, Shannon, years later.

Another nickname that I acquired was "Swan". The name was first given to me because I was the best wide receiver of my class during pickup football games, like Lynn Swann of the Pittsburgh Steelers. Later, after watching the movie "Warriors" with three of my classmates, this nickname became reinforced. Swan is the strong silent leader of the Warriors, the gang, and I was the strong silent leader of my friends.

Other movies that I remember watching in the theatre with my junior high school friends that have since then become classics are: "Grease," "Saturday Night Fever," "Star Wars," "The Blue Lagoon," "Rocky," "Alien," "Mad Max" and "The Exorcist." I regret seeing the last mentioned movie on this list and it is considered one of the scariest movies of all time.

Another "classic" moment in history that occurred during my junior high years was the "Blizzard of '79." During this event, so much snow piled up that it reached second floor windows. Garage roofs caved in (not ours, thank God) and we missed school for more than a week. When we did walk to school, snow was "knee deep" or more like "waist deep." I made some money snow blowing neighbors' sidewalks.

We had fun skitching, where we grabbed the bumpers of unsuspecting cars in the streets and took joyrides in the snow or ice. I do not see kids doing this anymore, maybe because they are all inside playing video games. I am glad I don't see kids skitching as it is very dangerous! The piles of snow did not melt for a long time, and there was still a trace of snow on the ground on May 1st.

*****

Starting in seventh grade, I started becoming not only an athlete, but also an avid sports fan and statistician. I read the sports section of the newspaper and collected baseball cards. Friends would try and fail to stump me in sports trivia. At one point, I knew every single player on the Major League Baseball (MLB) and National Hockey League (NHL) rosters, including their statistics and abilities, whether they were strong, fast, playmakers, goal scorers, or fighters.

I remember watching football, basketball or baseball games on TV while simultaneously listening to the Chicago Blackhawks games on the radio, reading the sports section of the newspaper and doing homework! I guess this marked my genesis as a multitasker, which I definitely consider myself today. I pondered a career as a sports journalist, but did not seriously look into this.

I also started listening to music in junior high school, and to this day, I can recall the songs and groups that were popular at the time. I fondly remember listening to "Bohemian Rhapsody," "We are the Champions" and other songs as hits for the first time. "Kung Fu Fighting" was also a popular song at that time, but it was released a little earlier, around the time that I first arrived in Chicago and did not understand English.

Decades later, when I would drive my daughter to her tennis tournaments, I would play a compilation of "motivational" songs to pump her up, and this included the songs I listed above plus "Killer Queen" and "Another One Bites the Dust." My daughter and I continued to bond over one of my favorite childhood bands when we she invited me to see the movie "Bohemian Rhapsody" with her.

My first concert that I attended was with my junior high colleagues, to see Shaun Cassidy! The boys were dragged to the concert by the girls. Because I was a dreamer who was shy, insecure, and very emotional, I developed a taste for "sappy love songs" including those by Barry Manilow, Air Supply, Chicago, and Journey. When I was in college, a taekwondo student of mine was surprised to see me studying while listening to these love songs in the background. Maybe he thought that I was too macho to listen to such sappy music.

As an adult, I attended a Barry Manilow concert with several female friends from junior high school. No male friends wanted to attend this concert this time. I guess they were not secure enough with their masculinity! I am proud to say that I have won several music ('70s and '80s) and sports trivia contests, usually on Caribbean cruises. Even though people were placed into groups for these contests, I was quickest to answer. I once even beat a family who were members of a '70s music band! Many of the songs from the late 70's and 80's are special and sentimental to me because they bring me back to my childhood. I remember exactly what I was doing when the songs played on the radio. I am extremely happy that a majority of my favorites have remained popular.

I also took piano lessons, like a stereotypical Asian, for a couple of years during junior high. I gave mandatory recitals, which included pieces by Beethoven and Bach. I hated to practice, so I never mastered this skill or that of the guitar (which I briefly learned later in life). If I could go back, I'd definitely have taken these lessons seriously. I would absolutely love to be able to pick up a musical instrument and "play it by ear."

I also never learned to sing, another skill I would love to have. I was able to sing "falsetto" and I used to entertain kids when I would sing "The Lion Sleeps Tonight" and songs by the Bee Gees or Frankie Valli and the Four Seasons. I had to stop singing falsetto later in life, because my voice would crack at times when I was treating patients. Since then I have not been able to reach any high notes.

In seventh grade, a very attractive and popular eighth grade girl, who was a student at my father's taekwondo school, expressed her interest in dating me. We started "going out" and talked to each other for hours on the phone (landlines of course). The song "Can't Smile Without You" by Barry Manilow became "our song." Because I was shy and insecure, I did not believe that a girl so pretty and popular could actually like me. This insecurity led to our eventual "break up." Unfortunately, I carried this insecure characteristic into high school.

*****

While struggling through elementary school, I restarted taekwondo lessons from my father, who owned two very successful studios on the northwest side of Chicago. I even became one of the instructors at the schools during high school.

Even though I was involved in taekwondo, which like all martial arts emphasizes self-discipline, I struggled with this character trait throughout high school. This was mainly because I also lacked self-esteem. I was "a dreamer but not a doer." I dreamed of being a professional athlete, initially a baseball player, then later a hockey player.

I was a great athlete who was naturally strong, fast and could jump. I was first or second in my class in push-ups, pull-ups and the bench press. I raced and tied a colleague who eventually became my high school's sprinter for the track team and received a college scholarship for track. I could almost touch the 10 foot basketball rim in high school. I dabbled in a few sports like baseball, hockey and gymnastics, but my lack of self-discipline and self-esteem resulted in a lack of perseverance and therefore I did not excel in any high school sport.

Even though my father acknowledged that my brother and I were naturally good athletes and martial artists (like my father), he discouraged us from having any serious thoughts of becoming professional athletes. He did not invest any money or time on training for us. Our family also lacked the financial resources for instruction, coaching or expensive equipment. I would have loved to have become a professional athlete, but my brother never voiced any such desire. While I may have had the athletic ability to "go pro," I lacked the discipline. I am glad that I was able to develop discipline later in life in academics, as part of God's plan to encounter other rewarding opportunities.

My father earned an eighth degree black belt in taekwondo, referred to as 8th dan (팔단) in Korean, and taught martial arts for the discipline and lifestyle. The tenets of taekwondo are: courtesy, integrity, perseverance, self-control and indomitable spirit. He did not like the sport or competition aspect of taekwondo because he believed that it brought out poor behavior, which contradicted the spirit of martial arts. Therefore, my brother and I seldom entered tournaments, even though when we did, we usually won first or second place trophies. I remember receiving a six foot trophy at one tournament after I beat a popular and favored instructor for the grand championship.

LIFE LESSON: Parents, instill in your children (and set examples from your lives) the personal characteristics that will allow them to grow into confident and successful children. Children, even though you may disagree and think that your parents don't understand you, realize that they want the best for you. By sacrificing for you, they make it possible for you to enjoy a better life than their own.

Chapter 4: Inheriting Values

My father was a leader in churches that we attended and later became a pastor when I was in college. He taught us the "fruits of the Spirit" that are listed in the Bible, as character traits for us to

---

[4] Me and my father (my TKD instructor), after I won first place at one of my first tournaments.

follow, alongside the tenets of taekwondo. These are: love, joy, peace, patience, kindness, goodness, faithfulness, gentleness and self-control.

My dad is a short Asian martial artist like Mr. Miyagi of the Karate Kid movies; he gave us lots of sage advice, like Miyagi. One of them was, "Don't chase money. Become good at what you do and money will naturally be rewarded to you."

He taught us related Biblical principles including, "The love of money is the root of all kinds of evil." "People who want to get rich fall into temptation and into foolish and harmful desires that plunge men into ruin and destruction." This principle applies to people who win the lottery or otherwise inherit a windfall, and then squander their millions. Many athletes and other entertainers are examples of this. If you do earn money, invest wisely and be very wary of get rich quick schemes.

It is indeed "better to give than to receive." Be generous to charities, friends and family but be wise in your giving. Do your research or ask about the charitable organizations before you donate.

My father always taught us that "We brought nothing into the world and we can carry nothing out." One thing I dislike is that too many physicians complain about their jobs. I believe that they went into their careers with the wrong motives. My daughter plans to follow my medical footsteps because she sees that I love what I do. Find a purpose, not a job.

Chapter 5: School of Hard Knocks

One month prior to starting high school, my brother and I attended a Cubs game. Even though I was a White Sox fan, I attended more

---
[5] My mom and me at my high school graduation

Cubs games than Sox games, because I grew up on the northside of Chicago. The Cubs play in Wrigley Field, on the northside.

While we were getting autographs from players during batting practice, I suddenly felt a sensation that I had never experienced, causing me to close my eyes. Then I felt someone placing a ball into my hand. I opened my eyes and saw that the Cubs left fielder (Ken Henderson), who placed the ball in my hand, had a worried look on his face, as did everyone else around me. I asked my brother, "What happened?" He said, "You just got hit in the face with that ball!"

I was taken by ambulance to the hospital that the Cubs players use, and I underwent reconstructive surgery to realign my left cheek (Zygomatic) bone, which had fractured in three places. Before the surgery, the anesthesiologist stuck something in my nose. I asked, "What is that?" He said, "Cocaine." I said, "What?!" He said, "Don't worry; you'll be asleep before you can get high on it!"

My face slowly healed before the start of high school, but to this day you can see and feel that my right cheekbone is more prominent than my left. What a way to start high school!

*****

I lacked discipline in both the academic and athletic arenas when I entered high school. Because my parents were immigrants, I received no guidance on what to expect as a freshman. At Lane Tech, you have to select an area of "concentration" similar to a major in college. Most students who plan to attend college choose math or science. Since I had no guide and I liked to draw, I chose art.

Unknown to me at the time, the art concentration entailed taking double period art classes for all four years, not leaving room in my schedule for subjects like history, physics and typing (yes, on typewriters). I had to take all of these subjects during summers, at high schools and junior colleges near my house. One of my art and homeroom classmates, Jill Soloway, later became a

Hollywood producer. She is famous for producing "Six Feet Under" on HBO and "Transparent" on Amazon Prime.

I earned primarily A's in math classes and obtained a score of 34 in the math section of the ACTs. I was even offered money for my answers to a final exam, by a student who later entered Chicago politics. No money exchanged hands!

I struggled in other classes, as symbolized by a composite ACT score of 24. My overall high school grade point average (GPA) was barely over 3.0, but by God's grace I was accepted from the waiting list into Wheaton College in Wheaton, Illinois. Wheaton College is nicknamed "the Harvard of Christian Colleges" and I would be the first to admit that my grades and ACT scores would not get me accepted today.

*****

There are some principles from Driver's Education at Lane Tech that I have applied throughout my life:

✓ "See the big picture."

- ✓ Don't just focus on the "car" in front of you, like the issue that is causing conflict between you and a friend, but try to see the big picture. Remember how important your friend is to you and consider the possible consequences before you make decisions.
- ✓ "Breathe." Taking a step back and deep breathing gives you clarity and peace of mind.
- ✓ Seeing the big picture has helped me in sports as well. A quarterback has to see as much of the field as possible before he makes a throw to avoid an interception. Same goes for a point guard in basketball, who has to see who is open for a pass or if he can drive to the basket or take a shot.
- ✓ "Leave yourself an out."
  - ✓ I try to have an "escape plan" when I'm in traffic or even in public places like restaurants and theatres.

- ✓ I also try to have "plan B" (and sometimes even plans C and D) when I make plans. This I do in case people "flake out" at the last minute, which is a too common occurrence. This strategy allows me to be less disappointed or waste time because of something that is out of my control.
- ✓ "Slower traffic keep right."
  - ✓ I wish all drivers, bikers, walkers, and people on escalators would obey this common courtesy. Disobedience of this "golden rule" is possibly responsible for many cases of road rage, including shootings on the expressways of Chicago.

LIFE LESSON: Hard work and discipline is more important than natural talent and intelligence.

Chapter 6: Self-esteem

Like many adolescents, I struggled with both self-esteem and self-discipline in high school. I hungered to be part of the cool and popular crowd, to be accepted, and feel like I belonged. I admit that I gave into peer pressure and drank alcohol on a few occasions during high school. Because I was shy and quiet, I liked the initial effects of alcohol, which decreases your inhibition. This allowed me to open up a little, but never act like a fool.

Many Asians lack one of the major enzymes that break down alcohol in your body called "aldehyde dehydrogenase." This makes us turn red when we drink and makes us "light weights," which I definitely am. Because of this, I did get drunk three times, all during the summer between my junior and senior years of high school. I hated the results of being drunk: lack of coordination of your muscles, poor response time, and not being in control of yourself.

The Bible does not condemn drinking alcohol and, in moderate amounts (1 to 2 drinks a day), it is actually good for your body. Abuse of alcohol is clearly against Biblical principles, against basic good judgement and shows lack of common sense for your health. I am glad that I recognized this while I was young.

This lesson led me to promise God never to become drunk again and I have kept my promise since then.

Because I lacked self- esteem, I placed everyone else above myself, whether it was their looks, talents or intelligence. One such person that I really admired was the salutatorian of my class. She was smart, attractive, and a great dancer. I've since learned that she earned her M.D. and PhD at an elite university in the United States. She was also unpretentious. She took the time to have telephone conversations with me on a couple of occasions about adolescent life and lent me some of her vinyl albums. Once, she even danced with me to "Love Me Tomorrow" by Chicago at a graduation party. I was too insecure and afraid to ask her out.

I considered pretty or popular girls "untouchable" and did not have the guts to approach them. One day in the cafeteria at Lane Tech, I made eye contact with my junior year homecoming queen. I approached her, talked to her, and obtained her home phone number, in spite of my crippling shyness. Eventually, after a couple of phone conversations, she realized how insecure I was and became disinterested. I was disappointed and reminded that I needed to work on my self-esteem.

There is some good news. Decades later, purely by happenstance, I ran into and engaged in conversations with my first "girlfriend" from junior high school. I also bumped into a former crush from Lane Tech. By that point, I had "morphed" into a confident young man and I was able to comfortably converse with them, without thinking they were too pretty or popular for me (nor that I was too popular for them). It was good to reminisce, catch up with childhood classmates and see how far I'd grown in my self-confidence.

LIFE LESSON: Girls are attracted to confident boys. This at least partly explains why so many good girls are attracted to bad boys.

LIFE LESSON: We are all created equal in the eyes of God. Yes, we have different roles in society, but no one is better than anyone else. Everybody suffers from at least some form of insecurity, and each person will express this in a unique way. Try to relate to everyone that enters your life; don't place people on pedestals and don't look down on others.

Chapter 7: Heaven on Earth

When I visited Wheaton College while I was still a student at Lane Tech high school, I thought that it was "heaven on earth." Even though Lane Tech is a great academic school, it is big (nearly 5000

---

[6] Playing DB for Wheaton College as a freshman

students) and people are always in a hurry, with no more than four minutes between classes.

By contrast, I saw Wheaton College students smiling and relaxed, strangers saying hi to each other, people going out of their way to help others and keeping one another accountable. I was initially disappointed when I was waitlisted by Wheaton, but unspeakably elated when I finally received my acceptance letter.

Before starting at Wheaton College, my father convinced me to study pre-medicine. Being a physician allows one the unique opportunity to help the needy and hurting anywhere in the world. This sounded like a noble goal. I remembered reading with admiration about Albert Schweitzer, a missionary physician to Africa. So, in spite of my doubts, I decided to give it my best effort to get into medical school.

During high school I dreamed of being popular but also down to earth. I wanted to be a great athlete but also a great student and a great person. In high school, star athletes were the most popular, especially football players. To relieve my curiosity about playing for a school's football team, I went out for the Wheaton College football team my freshman year, and was assigned to play defensive back.

Because every other player had played high school football, the coaches assumed that I knew what I was doing. I "learned on the job" very quickly, and I was rewarded with some playing time. I even had the opportunity to live out a fantasy where I hit a wide receiver hard as he was trying to make a catch, and my teammates applauded me for this highlight play.

I also got a taste of the risky aspect of football. During a scrimmage game with inmates of the Joliet Prison football team, I hit a huge (225 pounds) receiver. When I got up, I didn't know where I was. I managed to hang on to the receiver, while my teammates helped bring him down. Even though I suffered a mild concussion, I stayed in for the next play because my coaches did not realize that I "had my bell rung."

The relationships formed with teammates that became my role models was the best thing about playing football at Wheaton College. I had some classes with these players and soon realized that they were not exclusively great athletes, but also great students and great people. Aside from playing sports, they were involved in mission trips during vacations and ministries where they fed the homeless. Two of my teammates, twin brothers, after graduating from Wheaton College, became missionary pilots. They flew in much needed supplies to the impoverished country of Papua New Guinea. These teammates were indeed inspirational in helping me become a well-rounded student and person during college.

One memory that stands out involving a fellow football player occurred in French class. I always sat next to my teammate Steve, who later attended Yale medical school. One day, the professor returned the graded exams that the class had recently taken. She said that she was disappointed at how poorly everyone did, with the average being around 65. She didn't think that the exam was that hard, and neither did I. Nevertheless, I was hoping that I scored at least average.

When the professor handed the exam back to my football teammate, he had a big smile on his face, so I peeked at his test and saw that he received an 84. Finally, I received my exam and saw that I scored a 96! I didn't show it to my friend, and let him believe that he was the smartest in our French class. All of this was in friendly competition to motivate each other. Competition carries a negative connotation but it has provided me with motivation to push myself to succeed in academics and sports.

God blessed me with His grace in allowing me to be accepted into Wheaton College. This is where my development into a confident and disciplined young man began.

Chapter 8: Study Lessons

I did not study much in high school. Not only was I an immigrant learning a new language, I was the first born of immigrant parents who didn't know how to help me study in the American school system. But I mostly never learned good study habits because I lacked motivation and discipline. College was a transformative experience in learning what it took to become a physician.

As a pre-med student, I knew I would have to take certain science classes, but I was squeamish at the sight of "blood and guts." I even disliked touching worms and therefore did not like to fish. Nevertheless, I signed up for science classes that were required for my pre-med major.

Miraculously at Wheaton College, I very quickly "morphed" from never studying to studying all the time. Even when I was not studying, like during meals at the dining hall, I was planning what to study next. When I look back on the amount of time I spent studying, I am amazed by the sheer number of hours. I considered this period in my life (as well as medical school) as "purgatory", or in limbo, as I awaited my entry into "heaven" when I would become a physician. During this time I focused on patience (not giving into indulgences) until I was able to treat patients!

I quickly developed an effective and thorough study method. When I read my books or class notes, I first underlined important parts with a pencil. As I re-read the parts I underlined, I highlighted the more important parts with a yellow highlighter. Then, I re-read the areas that I had highlighted in yellow and I highlighted the *most* important parts with a pink highlighter. If I had time to read the "most important" parts again, I underlined the absolutely necessary parts with a red pen. With this method, I *only* had to remember the parts I marked in pink or red to prepare for exams or quizzes,! This system yielded good results.

It is important to turn to others for advice if learning a new skill, like studying. I was blessed to have helpful neighbors in my dorm during my freshman year, one of whom was Scott, a junior Philosophy major and fellow pre-med student. He was a straight A student, and after graduating from Wheaton College went on to receive his MD and PhD. Oh, he was also Korean! This was an incredible coincidence because there were less than ten Koreans and less than fifty Asians in the entire Wheaton College population.

Scott advised me, before I started my freshman classes, to collect all my syllabi and use them to put all of my future exams and papers that are due onto a calendar, so that I can plan for my semester ahead of time. This advice turned out to be invaluable, especially to a young adult who did not know how to study. Following his advice and by looking ahead in my calendar, I wrote my papers weeks before they were due. This allowed me to better prepare for exams that were scheduled at the same time as an assignment.

Speaking of papers, I took an English Literature class during the first semester of my freshman year. After my first exam, which consisted of mainly essay questions, I felt confident that I had given the "correct" answers. When I received my exam results, I saw that I received a C+ and I was puzzled. When I asked the professor what was wrong with my answers, he said, "Nothing, but they are not essays." I said, "What do you mean?" He realized after explaining why my answers were incomplete, that I had never learned how to write an essay when I was in high school! How was I even accepted into Wheaton College?

By the end of the semester, I learned how to write essays and I quickly improved my grades. One time, I remember that I paid a fellow student to type (yes, on a typewriter) my hand written paper so that I could study for other subjects. The paper received a poor grade, and my professor told me that it was because I did not correct my typing errors. I usually noticed errors when I typed my own papers before handing them in. I can proudly say that I received an A on every paper for the duration of my college career after this regrettable experience.

By my sophomore year, I discovered that I was smarter than I considered myself to be in high school. I realized that I understood concepts and started earning more A's than B's in classes that were difficult for other pre-med students. By the end of the sophomore year, the vast majority of the students who had started out "pre-med" had changed their minds. By the time we graduated, less than 20 out of the original 200 pre-med students applied to medical school.

I started to enjoy learning, even subjects that I would not have imagined, like music appreciation. I took Philosophy and Theology classes, and I decided to major in Religious Studies (the study of all major world religions), while taking the required pre-med courses.

After taking many theology courses, I arrived at the conclusion that I am a 4 ½ point Calvinist. I believe in four and possibly all five points of the acronym "TULIP." These letters stand for the following: Total depravity, Unconditional election, Limited atonement, Irresistible grace, and Perseverance of the saints. Since this is not a book about theology, I will ask the readers to look up TULIP or Calvinism if they want to know more.

I also read about the inspirational works of St. Augustine of Hippo, Thomas Aquinas, Anselm of Canterbury, Blaise Pascal, Socrates, and others. These humanities classes helped me to become the man I am today, by helping me to think clearly. The works I read helped me to give rational arguments for my beliefs and decisions. I made a flow chart of all of the major worldviews, philosophies and world religions to help me decipher the differences in each of these branches. The chart also helped me decide what I believe and why.

There are several lessons I learned when I was studying at Wheaton College and throughout my life. Organize your life and do not procrastinate. I have known many people with so much intelligence and talents who fail to live up to expectations: their own, their families', or their employer's. This failure is because they cannot organize their lives or because they are putting things off until the last minute. Create a "system" so that you do not get distracted by your disorganization or forgetfulness. Everyday tasks become less burdensome and overwhelming when you create an organized system that becomes automatic.

Here are some practical suggestions:

- Look behind you when you get up to leave to make sure that you did not leave anything behind, like your keys or phone. Check to see that you turned off car lights and closed the garage door as this prevents future problems.
- Make an inventory of your possessions (on paper, computer or at least in your brain.) Then try bringing less into your house or life than you take out.
- Organize your things into the following piles: "to keep," "to donate," and "to throw away." Live as simply as you can, because life gets more complicated as you get older.

- Don't throw your clothes on the floor. Either hang them up or put them in the laundry basket, even when you are tired after a long day of work.
- Put things back in their cases or packages after using them. This goes for CDs, DVDs, cereal and other food items.
- Don't let dishes piles up. Wash them right away after you eat and put them away. Find an organized place to leave them out to dry if you are going to use them soon.
- Make your bed every day. This simple task will make you feel like you are more organized and in control of your life, especially when you get home after a long day of work.
- Stay on top of your schedule and don't let tasks pile up. Set regular organizing times. Try to distract yourself from thinking the task is difficult, by

listening to music or podcasts. You can have the TV on in the background, as long as you don't stop your task to watch.

Try to create a "foolproof" of a system so that it becomes automatic. Hire or ask someone to keep you accountable, if you struggle in this area of life. Achieving a goal of an organized life will require hard work, but maintaining this system is much easier. As long as you have a system and do not fall back into old habits, you will be successful.

Chapter 9: Pranks and Prayer

During a break in the fall semester of my senior year, some friends and I went on a weekend retreat to "Honey Rock," a wooded property in Wisconsin owned by Wheaton College. While we were there, we relaxed, enjoyed nature and got away from studying for a

---

[7] Incognito as a ninja to pull pranks

bit. Four of us got "cabin fever" one night and we went around the camp looking for trouble.

We made ninja masks out of shirts and "borrowed" a chainsaw and flashlights from a nearby shed. We took off the chain and went around looking for "victims" to scare. We saw a couple by a fireplace. They were the perfect targets because they were out of touch with the world and staring into each other's eyes. We snuck up on them. We jumped in front of them and I shined the flashlight in their eyes, while my friends turned on the chainsaw. They started screaming and holding onto each other for dear life. We yelled, "Just joking!" and ran off. One of my friends knew the young woman we scared, and he said that she was a good sport about it. Fortunately, we did not get in any trouble.

Wheaton College students sometimes pulled some great pranks. In biology class, we had to dissect fetal pigs. The snouts of the pigs looked like mushrooms, so some students took these and placed them in the salad bar of the cafeteria. Some students took methylene blue from their chemistry labs and put it in the punch in the cafeteria. This created a long line at the student health center, because students were worried that their urine was green in color.

Wheaton College is a Christian college and everyone is required to attend chapel. During services in chapel there were numerous pranks. One of the highly entertaining pranks involved some students climbing onto the roof of the chapel and somehow parachuting lab mice through the lights in the ceiling, onto the seated students.

Overall, chapel was a great experience. I was privileged to have had the opportunity to listen to great speakers, including Billy Graham (Wheaton College's most famous alumnus), Chuck Colson, Francis Shaffer, Josh McDowell, and Luis Palau (whose twin sons were my dorm neighbors one year). George H. W. Bush spoke in chapel as a commencement speaker my sophomore year. Years later, Todd Komarnicki, a playwright, director and producer, who graduated with me from Wheaton College, was selected to be a chapel speaker. Todd's most popular production has been the movie "Alf."

Even the hardest working students and employees need diversion in their lives. Finding fun activities that don't hurt other people or yourself can bring needed stress relief to hard workers.

Chapter 10: College: Purgatory

Unfortunately, because I was studying all the time, I did not have an active social life and I adopted two theme songs: "I am a Rock, I am an Island" by Simon and Garfunkel and "Another Saturday Night (and I Ain't Got Nobody)" by Sam Cooke. Sad, huh?

Sometimes on Friday nights during my freshman year, after I unsuccessfully tried to study, I instead watched "Friday Night Videos." I remember being enamored with videos that are now classics like, A-ha's "Take On Me," Wham's "Careless Whispers," and Duran Duran's "Hungry Like The Wolf" and "Union of the Snake," when they were hits for the first time. The MTV channel actually played music videos back then! Starting my junior year, I switched to watching "Knight Rider," "A-Team" and "Miami Vice" on Friday nights. Again, sad, huh?

Somehow, I did go on a handful of dates. My most memorable dates were watching "The Karate Kid" (the original, not the one with Jackie Chan and Jaden Smith), "The Gods Must Be Crazy," and "The Last Dragon," which are some of my all-time favorite movies. I also remember going on a "blind date" with a six foot tall young lady. Later, she ended up becoming one of my taekwondo students. Her brother, Donn Nelson, became my most famous Wheaton College taekwondo student.

Speaking of "The Karate Kid," one of my favorite principles that I have applied to my life, and also advise everyone to do, comes from this movie: "Balance, Daniel San, balance." This principle is the secret to leading a healthy lifestyle. People ask me what my secret is to staying fit, as I weigh and basically look the same as I did in high school. I initially joke with them and say that I've been on a secret diet all my life, a "see food diet," that I eat everything I see. When they ask me to explain, I tell them the real secret is "balance."

I prescribe my patients "Vitamin D." The "D" stands for discipline. I do not advocate any extreme diets, pills or even exercise programs that cannot be continued for the rest of their lives. It's hard work to regain fitness if you let yourself go, but once you reach your goal, maintenance is *much* easier.

Try to keep things simple and manageable: weight loss occurs if you burn more calories than you consume; weight gain occurs in the opposite way. You gain muscle, the only good source of weight gain, by exercising and not by consuming supplements. There is no magic pill or protein shake to get a lean, muscular body.

I tell my patients that exercise is not about a gym membership or equipment, but rather one's will and motivation. Try to take the stairs instead of the elevator. Walk, jog or bike instead of using a car or public transportation for short trips. Do some form of exercise, 5 – 6 days a week if possible, even for small amounts. Exercise, not necessarily medications, is the solution for back pain, arthritis or even emotional pain like depression and anxiety.

Most people hire personal trainers because they lack motivation, not because they don't know what to do. You can exercise in your house, a hotel room, or on vacation with little to no equipment. For example; you can do push-ups against the wall, use a Thera band for strengthening or stretching, practice yoga or do Pilates. You can even kick or run in place in any room; just don't knock over any precious items!

When I returned from my first European vacation after seven weeks away, my brother asked me, "Did you lift while you were there?" He was surprised that I looked the same as before I left. I said, "No, I did push-ups and pull-ups at parks, and I walked a lot." I do not gain weight or get out of shape over the holidays and vacations, so I don't let my patients use that excuse. Remember, "Balance!"

When I took study breaks in college, I enjoyed participating in some form of exercise. Besides occasionally weight lifting, I played intramural sports, specifically volleyball and basketball. At my strongest point, I could bench press 280 pounds while weighing 140 pounds.

During my senior year, I played on an intramural volleyball team that we named "Global Gang" because the team members were from all over the world (Latin America, Africa and Asia).

Most of these international students grew up as "MKs" (missionaries' kids). I guess it was destiny that I would later be involved in a world-renowned video game with the same acronym, "MK"! Our team had a great group of "characters" and we easily succeeded in "kombat," winning the intramural championship trophy.

During my freshman year, two students who were part of Wheaton College's "Karate Club" asked me to start and instruct a

---

[8] My WC TKD students: Donn Nelson being kicked by a Philosophy professor

Taekwondo Club, my sophomore year. I agreed, so they disbanded the Karate Club. These two colleagues helped me with a demonstration, and 40 people (students and professors) immediately enrolled as new taekwondo students. My favorite part of Taekwondo Club demonstrations was performing the "flying side kick" over 8 – 10 people to break boards, as I had "demonstrated" against my childhood bully. Over the next three years, I taught numerous students and faculty members, including a future Olympic athlete (Nancy Swider Peltz Jr.) and an NBA coach and general manager (Donn Nelson). After I left Wheaton College, I went on to teach taekwondo to some professional athletes, specifically hockey players from the Chicago Blackhawks.

*****

One day while eating lunch with a fellow pre-med student at Wheaton College, I witnessed him fretting over the amount of food the server at the cafeteria had given him when he went back for seconds. I said, "Just leave it." I guess, over the years, I had forgotten how I had valued food while growing up in Korea. He said that he had a principle of not wasting anything on his plate. This made an immense impression on me and I adopted it; I practice it to this day. Since then, I have expanded this principle and I try not to waste *anything*: time, talent or energy.

I have some other interesting stories related to my dining experience at Wheaton College. My tastes were not of an average American. I lived in Korea until age eight, and then with my family until I enrolled at Wheaton College at eighteen years of age. I did eat some American meals, but mostly grew up eating Korean food. One day I went to get milk for my cereal. All other milk was gone so I saw and tasted skim milk for the first time. I said to my colleague who was with me that there is something wrong with the milk dispenser. He said, "No, that's how skim milk is." I grew up drinking whole milk, and I had never tasted any other type of milk.

I disliked skim milk then, but since then I have changed my tastes and dislike the taste of any fat in my milk.

Not only did I grow up drinking whole milk, but I also ate some form of meat (or at least eggs) at every meal. Once, I was "forced" to eat grilled cheese with tomato soup for dinner and I felt like I hardly had anything to eat. Again, this perception that meals need to involve meat has changed, and now such a meal would definitely be satisfying.

At Wheaton College, I tasted some very typical American food for the first time, including chicken pot pie, pot roast, meatloaf, Brussel sprouts, and corn dogs. I still have not tasted deep fried desserts (Twinkies, Snickers or Ice Cream) and I do not understand how these can taste good. In general, "carnival food" is not only bad for you but, in my opinion, bad tasting!

I try to continue to try new foods, and I am not afraid to try any food for the challenge or cultural edification. My daughter and I have met Andrew Zimmern and have told people that I could eat everything he eats on his TV show, "Bizarre Foods." During my travels after graduating from Wheaton College, I have tasted bugs, elephant shrews and live octopus tentacles.

I remember that growing up I constantly had food on my mind. If I did not eat every two or three hours, I was starving! After football practice at Wheaton College, I felt famished and I usually ate seconds, thirds and fourths of the main course (as well as the salad, soup and dessert.) One day, I was so hungry that I went back for my *seventh* serving of pork chops! I can no longer eat as much, but people are still amazed how much I eat and still look fit. They ask, "Where do you put it all?" That is when I tell them about my "see food diet" and "balance."

College life can be fun, even for the very serious and dedicated students. While I wish that I could have experienced even more enjoyable moments during my college career, I am thankful for the fond memories created at Wheaton College.

Chapter 11: Global Perspective

During my senior year spring break at Wheaton College, I went on my first mission trip to a remote mountainous village in Honduras, Central America. At this time, Honduras was the second poorest

---

[9] Digging trenches to lay pipes for a water system in a remote Honduran village

country in the Western Hemisphere by income per capita; Haiti was the worst. We volunteered in a village that had no electricity and no running water. We dug trenches to install a gravity fed water system to supply drinking water to the families of this village.

After working hard during the day, one of my favorite "extracurricular" activities was giving a taekwondo demonstration with two other members of the mission team, who were my students in the Wheaton College Taekwondo Club. One of the acts during the demo was breaking bricks that we were using to build the water tank that would hold the water that subsequently flowed to each home via pipes that we laid.

Another highlight of this trip was finding and trapping a scorpion in a Coke bottle (years before it was a Mortal Kombat character), packing it in my duffle bag and bringing it back to my dorm to keep as a pet for the rest of the school year. I fed it grasshoppers and crickets a few times a week. When I traveled to

Europe after graduating from college, I asked my sisters to feed it. They did not do this and it was stiff (dead) when I returned. On a subsequent trip to Honduras, this time to the jungles of La Mosquitia, I saw a tarantula eating a vampire bat in my bathroom. I trapped both in a jar with the plan to bring them back to the United States, but the tarantula died, after devouring the bat.

Before my first mission trip, I did not speak Spanish. I had studied two semesters of French in college and spoke fluent Korean, but had never studied Spanish whatsoever. I thought that I would be fine, since the trip was for a week over spring break. Instead, I was *very* frustrated that I could not communicate with the Hondurans. I promised myself that before returning to Honduras I would learn Spanish.

One month before returning for my second trip, I taught myself Spanish by studying my sister's Spanish 101 book and then practicing it with Hondurans. Language is typically easily learned through "immersion" and I eventually became fluent in Spanish because I regularly returned to Honduras on mission trips and utilized the language. I subsequently began working in Chicago, where I started to speak Spanish everyday with my patients, without a translator.

After seeing how "dirt poor" people of Honduras live, I was reminded how I had lived in a developing country during the first eight years of my life, albeit not nearly as impoverished. Like the majority of Americans, I slowly became desensitized to this and started contributing to the incredible amount of "waste" that Americans throw away, especially when it comes to leftover food. I am thankful that I regained my global perspective by going on these mission trips and learning from the people I met.

Thirty years after my first mission trip to Honduras, I revisited this village with my daughter. I wanted to show her the impact that students can have during short term mission projects. The village that we helped by installing a water system, providing water to each house, is now thriving as a result. This farming village had dramatically "morphed." They were barely surviving by selling their crops in city markets while sharing their profits with middle men (called "coyotes" in Spanish).

As a result of the water system, they earned enough to purchase their own trucks and other vehicles, no longer needing the "coyotes." They negotiated with Walmart to sell their crops in their stores, which brought an increase in their earnings. They experienced benefits that they had never imagined, like being able to send their own children to bilingual schools. It was extremely rewarding and heartwarming to be able to see this progress and share the long-term results of mission trips with my daughter.

Chapter 12: Gap Year

I had a great experience at Wheaton College, and I wholeheartedly believe that I would not have been able to turn my life around and get into medical school if I had not attended Wheaton. I tell people that I did not become a doctor because of myself, but that God allowed me to become one *in spite* of myself. He completely transformed me while I was there.

---

[10] Neuschwanstein Castle, Germany

Nevertheless, I was burned out from studying all the time for four years, including during my vacations. After I was accepted into my first-choice medical school, the University of Illinois College of Medicine, I was granted a one year deferment (now called gap year). During this year, I traveled, trained, and taught a lot of taekwondo.

Shortly after graduating from Wheaton College, I traveled to Europe with one of my college roommates for that summer, backpacking and getting to know different countries and cultures. Walking through red-light districts, visiting clothing-optional beaches, and learning about some countries' very open attitudes regarding sex was shocking to a kid who grew up very naïve. A situation of culture shock occurred while strolling the beach in Nice. I was chatting with some local women on the French Riviera beach and they suggested a "menage-a-trois." I declined.

Overall, my first European trip was very pleasant, as I was able to visit and see world-renowned historical buildings, museums, paintings and statues. These included: the Eiffel Tower and the Louvre (where the Mona Lisa is located) in Paris; the Leaning Tower of Pisa; the Vatican and Sistine Chapel in Rome; the David statue in Florence; Mozart's house and the castle from the movie "Sound of Music" in Austria; "Guernica," the huge painting by Picasso in Spain; and the Berlin Wall in East Berlin before it was destroyed. By the way, while admiring the "David" statue, I realized that Michelangelo (the sculptor and painter, not the Ninja Turtle) did not accurately represent Jewish culture when he inaccurately sculpted a certain body part on David.

This trip instilled in me the "travel bug" to visit as many parts of the world as possible. I also became very independent while abroad. I traveled alone for part of the trip, and I splurged on *one* phone call to my parents during my seven weeks in Europe. I should have at least called to remind my sisters to feed my scorpion! I did not tell my family when I was returning to Chicago, and I simply showed up at home one day! Of course, this was all before email and social media.

A few months later, I returned to Honduras, where I traveled around the country with another college roommate on his motorcycle. I became very familiar with this third world country during this road trip. As I have previously mentioned, I taught myself Spanish and practiced it with Hondurans while I was there. I saw poor villages and extreme poverty in the city, but I also enjoyed the coast for a bit. I even won second place in a beach volleyball tournament with my friend and a Honduran player.

Prior to this trip, I assumed that everyone in developing countries was poor; I did not know that there was such a *huge* disparity between the rich and the poor. Years later, a sixteen year old Honduran who stayed with my family when he visited Chicago had the opposite impression of the United States. He assumed that everyone in America was rich. When I drove him through parts of

Chicago where I work and my patients live, he said, "This doesn't even look like the USA!"

*****

Besides teaching at his own schools, my father taught taekwondo classes that students took for college credit at DePaul University. During my gap year, I took over and taught this class for him. I also trained with elite taekwondo athletes, some of whom became national champions, including Arlene Limas, who earned a gold medal at the 1988 Olympics in South Korea. Others competed in the Olympics in other sports, namely Powerlifting (Jeff Michels 1988, 1992) and Speed Skating (Nancy Swider Peltz, Jr. 2010).

Towards the end of my sabbatical year, I taught private lessons to my first Chicago Blackhawks hockey player, Troy Murray. Troy had a long NHL career with the Blackhawks and other teams, and has served as a radio commentator for Hawks games since his retirement. Cross training in martial arts is very helpful for athletes, by improving various aspects of athletics, including concentration, discipline, hand-eye coordination and flexibility.

    This gap year provided me with a necessary break from the hard work I put in at Wheaton college. I am extremely glad that I made this decision. It cultivated other aspects of my life that have played significant roles in providing me abundant joy throughout my career as a physician. I am also grateful for meeting and networking with great people during this break from my studies.

Chapter 13: Hittin' the Books

Medical school at the University of Illinois, Champaign-Urbana, was another eye-opening experience. I had attended a small Christian liberal arts college, and now I was on the campus of a huge public university. The curriculum was rigorous, with students taking nine courses during the first semester and ten classes in the second semester.

I enjoyed Gross Anatomy (not the movie) and learning the realistic details of our bodies by dissecting a human corpse for the first time. We learned the names of every part of the human body from our textbook "Gray's Anatomy," not from the TV show "Grey's Anatomy." My pre-med studies and experiences in Honduras "morphed" me from a squeamish teenager and desensitized me to potentially nauseating situations.

By the time I was a medical student, the administration had become very strict about the handling of cadavers, people who gave their bodies to science. For example, the anatomy lab was closed on Halloween to prevent pranks from happening. I heard about past medical students who placed their corpse on a toilet and turned off the bathroom lights, to scare the overnight custodian.

There were two exams per semester, and each exam was an all-day event covering all nine or ten classes. If you failed one subject during the year, you could retake it over the summer. If you still did not pass, or if you failed two subjects during the year, you had to repeat the entire academic year. Three of my classmates repeated their first year and only one of them ultimately passed. This scenario reminds me of a joke:

Q. "What do you call the medical student that graduates last in their class?"

A. "Doctor!"

This joke demonstrates that as long as you are committed to achieving your goal, you can become a physician.

In spite of the heavy class load, I took a teaching assistant position for freshman Chemistry students during my second semester. The role not only taught me leadership, but helped pay for my tuition. Needless to say, this was a *very* busy time in my life.

I did have to take study breaks, so I exercised at the campus gym. While doing some martial arts there, I met and sometimes trained with Ho Sung and Ho Young Pak. They were Wu-Shu practitioners, so their styles were different from taekwondo.

Nevertheless, there was enough crossover to allow some sparring with each other.

Another diversion was attending occasional "Fighting Illini" basketball games at the university. I admired the basketball players' dedication to training whenever I saw them at the gym, and some of them went on to have prominent professional careers in the NBA. This Illini team was favored to win the national championship that year and reached the "Final Four." In the semi-finals they played the University of Michigan Wolverines, whom they had easily beaten twice in the regular season.

Some fellow students and I decided that this game was too important to miss, so we decided not to study that night. Unlike the regular season games that the Illini had easily won, this game was very close and each team had the lead several times. Unfortunately, our team lost this nail biting game in the last second. My friends and I were crushed! Oh well, back to studying.

The first year of medical school was the busiest year of my life. I am glad that I had developed good study habits in college, so that I was able to enjoy some extracurricular activities and meet people who would play significant roles in my martial arts career.

Chapter 14: Adversity in Africa

During my summer break between my first and second year of medical school, I went on another mission trip, bringing along one of my classmates. We traveled to Zaire (now known as Democratic Republic of the Congo). I asked John to accompany me because he was a smart but very sincere and extremely sympathetic young

---

[11] With Masai Warriors in Africa

man. We talked about life, from sports to music to serious issues, while studying together.

When we were in Zaire, we often sang the song "Africa" by Toto. John thought that part of the song was "There's nothing that a hundred men *on mars* could ever do." We playfully changed the words from "I bless the rains down in Africa" to " I catch the rays down in Africa" and "Don't catch the AIDS down in Africa."

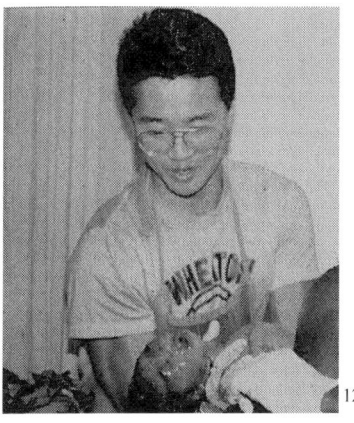

I helped in the delivery of one young woman's child. Having her baby named after me, "Philippe" in French, was one of the highlights from this trip.

---

[12] Delivering "Philippe" in Zaire

During one procedure, we were suddenly disturbed by the sound of a chicken as it stumbled into the operating room, looking for scraps. When I shared this humorous event with my friends who had also been on mission trips, one shared his own story. A vulture perched itself on one of the operating room windows and watched the doctors intently, as it was common for windows to lack screens in impoverished countries. While the birds may have been shooed away hungry, I was fed many unusual treats. During my trip, I tasted termites, a delicacy when they are in season, and an elephant shrew, a rodent about the size of a rabbit.

We met "Pygmies" who stood three feet tall as adults. I learned that certain people did not want their photos taken because they feared that their souls would be captured by the camera. This was years before the Mortal Kombat character, Shang Tsung, started capturing souls. Once, to be friendly, I approached a group of children and they ran away screaming. I hope that this was not because they thought I was going to eat them (or steal their souls). Talk about "stranger danger!"

Many people believed in animism and magic. Disagreements sometimes broke out over accusations of a villager placing a curse on someone else. Even those that believed in modern medicine also believed in spells. For example, if an individual suffered appendicitis, friends or family brought the patient for surgical treatment. They blamed the reason for appendicitis on an enemy putting a curse on that patient.

In one village, I learned that in its tribal language there is one word for non-blacks (no distinction between Asians, Europeans), one word for Africa, and one word for "the place where non-blacks come from." While there are many tribal languages, Swahili is one of the common languages of the nation and French is the official language for government and education. I learned some Swahili words and phrases like "Jambo!" (hello) and "Asante sana" (thank you very much) from the locals. I would hear these words again decades later, when I watched "The Lion King" movie with my daughter. The popular phrase, "Hakuna Matata" (no worries) was not something I ever learned in Africa.

Some of the local high schoolers, who were learning English as part of the "English Club," asked me if John and I were twins! How they thought a Caucasian and Asian could be twins was mind-blowing. One of the missionaries told us that she could get neighborhood boys to perform minor chores by giving them cold water from the fridge. The things we take for granted in the United States!

In spite of cultural differences and living in a remote area, a decent number of the African villagers knew about Bruce Lee and Jackie Chan. They correctly assumed that I was a martial artist and asked me to be a guest instructor at their "Karate Club." After I taught some techniques that they had not seen, I sparred the instructor. Unfortunately, he was not used to my kicks, so he "ran into" a tornado kick with his left eyebrow, which I subsequently sutured. Oops!

*****

After our mission trip, my friend and I decided to visit Zambia and Zimbabwe before returning home. We went on a safari in Hwange National Park and saw animals in their natural habitat, that I had previously only seen on the Discovery or National Geographic channels. I was amazed by the diversity at the park:

---

[13] My friend John at the Victoria Falls

lions, cheetahs, rhinos, hippos, elephants, giraffes, buffaloes, zebras and antelopes.

    We also got to visit one of the world's greatest marvels, Victoria Falls. After looking at this splendor from above, we decided to find a path from which we could look up at the falls. What we found instead was a path that kept getting more and more narrow and steep until we finally found it unsafe to go any further.

    While standing and contemplating our next move, all of a sudden I saw John slip and fall. He tumbled rapidly down the steep rocks until he was too far for me to see. A group of climbers were nearby and helped search for John but they only found broken netting. They assumed his body broke through the netting and this was confirmed later. It was shocking and tragic, to say the least. That night I cried for the first time in years, and slept with the lights on. The next day, God gave me the strength to call the American Embassy, relocate to the ambassador's house, and extend my stay in Africa until I could identify my friend's body. He was eventually found in the waters below Victoria Falls.

The ambassador called John's family but nobody picked up. He then called my family, but my father misunderstood the ambassador and initially thought that I had died because of his limited English. My dad was reassured when I called him later from the embassy. When I returned from Africa and met him at the airport, he gave me a little hug, for the first time in my life that I could recall. In my experience, many Asian men are very stoic, especially martial artists.

After I returned to the United States, I met John's family and we have remained friends over the years. I attended John's funeral; years later, I also attended his parents' funerals. I have also been to some family birthdays, weddings, graduations, Christmas and Thanksgiving parties.

At one Thanksgiving party, I almost amputated the tip of my daughter's finger as I was closing a door, when she was 17

d. John's sister drove us, as fast as an ambulance would, to the nearest hospital. My daughter underwent emergency surgery, and she has healed completely fine. Thank you Lord.

I can still vividly remember when John died. It could easily have been me. Up to that point in my life, his was the only tragic death that I had experienced. Rest in peace, my friend.

LIFE LESSON: Life is short. Embrace and enjoy every second of life you have. Say, "I love you" and show how deeply you cherish your loved ones. "God works in mysterious ways" and this does not always seem fair to human minds. Nevertheless, try to live in peace within your own heart and mind, as well as with your friends, family and anyone else who enters your life.

[14]

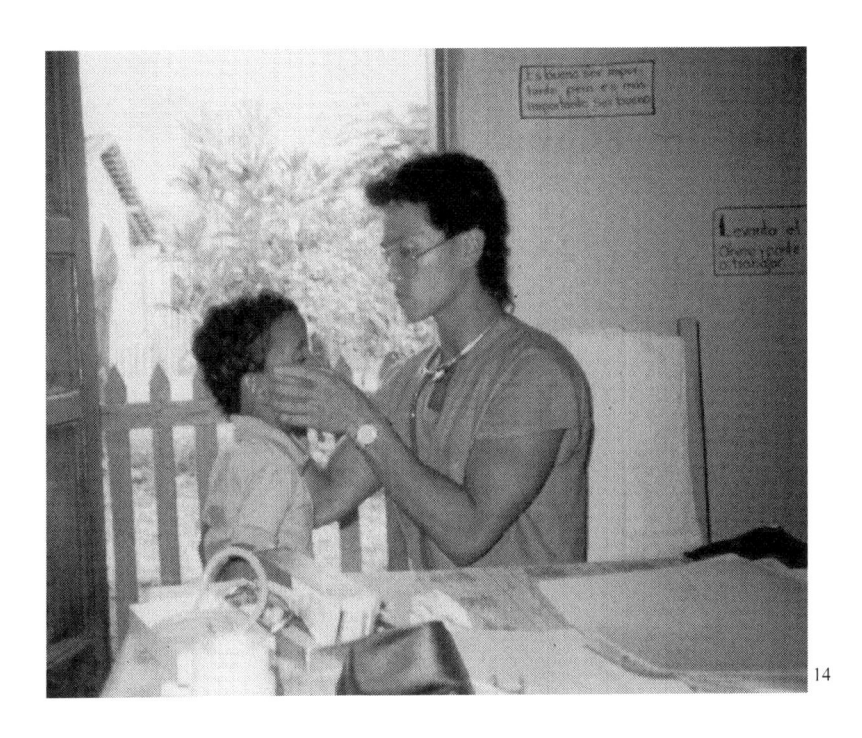

Chapter 15: Rockford Files

The University of Illinois College of Medicine has four campuses: Chicago, Champaign-Urbana, Peoria and Rockford. Students either attend classes at the Chicago campus for four years, or attend the Champaign-Urbana campus their first year. If you choose Champaign-Urbana, you stay there, or you can choose to complete

---

[14] Treating a Honduran boy during one of my med school rotations

the next three years at the Peoria or Rockford campus. I chose Rockford.

During my medical school years, "Doogie Howser, M.D." was a popular TV show, about a child prodigy that became a physician. Because I looked young to my patients, some called me "Doogie." Many other patients would also call me this after medical school, during residency and even during my practicing career.

Many memories from medical school at Rockford stand out; I will share some of the highlights. Every class has several cut throat students who always want to score the highest on the exams. Most of them want to enter subspecialties like: plastic, orthopedic or neurosurgery. One day, I was studying with a fellow student. He was racking his brain because he and another colleague (they both became surgeons after graduation) could not figure out who scored the highest on a pathology exam. When I admitted that it was me, he was shocked, perhaps because he knew that I did not have the same goals as they did.

During medical school, I rotated through several specialties and subspecialties, including general, neuro and cardiovascular surgery. It is common that medical students faint or feel light headed when they are exposed to the operating room for the first time. It was rumored that a student in a previous class fainted into a patient's open abdomen, while holding retractors during an operation. I thank God that I did not feel queasy whatsoever during my surgeries or other procedures. I had come a long way from the kid who wouldn't touch worms!

Some eye opening moments in the operating room (O.R.) included seeing my first open heart surgery. By my second such surgery, I became bored and couldn't wait for this long procedure to end. I remember hearing the hammer and chisel sounds during orthopedic and neurosurgeries, including those involving the neck and spine. It sounded like men working on a railroad, and the song, "Chain Gang" by Sam Cooke kept playing in my mind.

During the neurosurgery rotation, I saw a patient after a motorcycle accident, in which he slid under an 18 wheel truck at a high speed. He suffered a shearing injury, in which all parts of the front of his body were sliced off, including his nose and his penis. This image is one of the reasons why I do not ride motorcycles.

One surgeon said to me, after a nurse told him that students were being orientated to the operating room, "If you get orientated, do you get slanted eyes?" I said, "No, you become smarter!" Everyone in the O.R. laughed. I am sure surgeons would get in trouble if they made such racial jokes today, I would hope.

I remember the first time I delivered a baby in Rockford. Good thing that I was in a mask and gown, because when the patient started to push, I felt her urine hit me like a powerful water gun! I was once squirted by a newborn boy as well, when I was examining him. I have learned my lesson and now I examine male babies from the side.

Other obstetrics memories include our group performing the *third* cesarean section on a sixteen year old girl. The obstetrician who performed that particular c-section, normally a grumpy old man, told the same joke to every group of students that rotated with him. He would ask, "What is the main thing that you need to remember about dyspareunia?" The term dyspareunia means pain during intercourse. Students would shout out very scientific answers and he would shoot them all down, saying, "No, no, no." Finally he would answer, "The main thing that you have to remember about dyspareunia, is that dyspareunia is better than no pareunia at all!" Then he would laugh out loud to himself.

*****

While attending medical school, I had the opportunity to do rotations in Kenya, Africa, and in the jungles of La Mosquitia in Honduras. Patients I treated in each place were similar in terms of illnesses, including diabetes, hypertension and common respiratory infections. In many ways, they had the same medical troubles as my American patients. Of course, I also treated conditions that you don't see in the States, like malaria and parasitical diseases. Some people complained of vomiting worms or seeing worms in their feces. I also saw renal or cardiac diseases that were complications of untreated strep bacterial infections; you don't normally see these conditions in the United States anymore because of antibiotics.

I did not get sick in Kenya and was even able to enjoy a safari and meet the Masai warriors in the Serengeti. I, regrettably, did get sick in La Mosquitia. Being sick in the jungle is not fun and I longed for the days when I was sick at home, with a TV, refrigerator, and my mom to take care of me. When I sat on the toilet in La Mosquitia, I had so much watery diarrhea that I could not tell whether I was urinating or defecating! Going to the bathroom was also an adventure, as that is where I caught the tarantula eating the vampire bat.

*****

The most memorable experience of my medical school career occurred during my Psychiatry rotation. A female patient was admitted because she was displaying erratic behavior and suffering from insomnia. She believed that her body was occupied by another spirit. Her voice changed back and forth from a female to a male voice during my intake exam. During this interview, I remembered Biblical stories that my dad told us when we were growing up, about Jesus and his disciples casting out evil spirits from people.

Since the patient had not been sleeping, she was drifting in and out as she responded to my questions. Suddenly, she jolted up and came towards me. I made a mistake by sitting in the corner and I could not escape as she stood over me.

This patient, in the male voice, shouted "I possess [her name] and I can possess you too!" I stared straight into her eyes and clearly said, "No, you can't. I have the Holy Spirit inside me and It is stronger than you." By this time, the patient had become so loud that one of the social workers came into her room. The patient turned away from me, returned to her normal self, and wept like a baby.

I rounded on this patient every day. The psychiatrist started her on medications upon admission. One week after our initial exam, I said to this patient, "You seem to be doing a lot better. What do you think happened?" She said, "I think the medications are helping, but to be honest, since you did whatever you did when you first interviewed me, I felt the male spirit leave my body."

I told the patient exactly what happened and I prayed with her. She was extremely grateful. I will leave it up to the readers to decide whether I performed an "accidental" exorcism or if the patient improved because of her medications.

LIFE LESSON: "Visualize it," "be ready for anything" and "expect the unexpected." Everybody knows the biblical story of "David versus Goliath". David was a young shepherd boy who was thrust into battle against this giant because everyone else was afraid. But he was ready and willing, thus achieving greatness. Be David, not Goliath.

A modern example of being "David" includes Eric Semborski, who was summoned to be the backup goalie for the Blackhawks after their starting goalie suffered appendicitis. There was no time for the Hawks' minor league goalie to arrive in time for the game. Semborski was a recreational player with a "normal job" but when thrust into this crucial situation, he was ready and willing.

Another example of successfully taking on a sudden situation is a man who had no CPR training but saved a woman's life by performing CPR to the rhythm of the song "Staying Alive." He had remembered a scene in a TV show where characters practiced CPR to this song.

"Some people are born great, some people achieve greatness, and some people have greatness thrust upon them."

Chapter 16: Taking the Hippocratic Oath

Being exposed to the various specialties made me contemplate becoming something other than a family practitioner, but ultimately I chose to stick with what I imagined doing when I first thought of becoming a physician. Years later, when I was on a medical mission trip with some anesthesiologists and

---

[15] Me as commencement speaker, with my 7th grade teacher (left) and new principal of Reinberg elementary school

119

gynecologists, I felt like a specialist because they came to *me* with a variety of questions. When friends say to me, "Can I ask a medical question?", I jokingly reply, "I'm not a psychiatrist!"

While studying in Rockford, I received news about Ho Sung and Ho Young Pak, the brothers with whom I sometimes trained at Champaign-Urbana. They had been recruited to become the stunt doubles of the Teenage Mutant Ninja Turtles (TMNT) movies! I felt proud for my friends but did not think twice about disrupting my medical school career to pursue Hollywood. Later that year, I was considered to be a model for the home exercise machine, "Soloflex," but was ultimately not selected.

*****

I finished medical school in 1992 and received my M.D. which stands for Doctor of Medicine. My graduating class from the University of Illinois College of Medicine - Rockford had 35 students. An interesting fact is that two of them were in the same home room with me at Lane Tech High School! The really amazing fact is that none of us were good or great students at Lane, but somehow turned around in college and eventually became physicians!

---

[16] Med school graduation with two high school classmates from our home room

Upon graduating, I quickly felt the prestige of being a physician. At my 10th year high school reunion, one of my former locker partners very frankly said, "Out of everyone here that became doctors, I didn't think you would be one of them!" I laughed and agreed with him.

I felt honored when I was invited to be the commencement speaker at the eighth grade graduation of my last elementary school. This invitation came from the same teacher who wrote in my yearbook that I would need good luck in high school! Unknown to me at that time, this event was a foreshadowing of things to come.

After medical school, I returned to Korea for the first time since I immigrated to Chicago. During this trip, I visited my relatives, whom I had not seen since I left as an eight year old, and I visited my family's old house and toured my kindergarten. I also tasted local cuisine, including live octopus tentacles. The server cuts and serves the tentacles to you while they are still moving. You put each of them in your mouth and consume the tentacle,

---

[17] Back in Korea in 1992, with a Korean lady wearing a traditional Hanbok dress

feeling it move around in your mouth. This experience is something you now see on shows like "Bizarre Foods."

    I also became familiar with Korean pop music, which is now very popular all over the world. Since returning to the United States, I have not kept up with K-pop music. Whenever I attend "K fests" (Korean Festivals) in Chicago, I'm amazed how well non-Koreans can sing and rap Korean music.

    It may be different now, but when I visited Korea in 1992, societal norms were expected to be followed. You were looked upon as weird if you deviated from strictly followed behavior. One example of this took place when I attended a baseball game, in 90°F (32°C) weather. People stared at me because I was wearing a tank top, shorts and sunglasses. Most adults were in shirts and pants, some with ties, at a baseball game!

    Even though Korea had "morphed" into a rich nation, I was glad to have grown up in America, because I got the impression that in Korea everyone looked, acted and thought the same. In spite of the conformity, I was impressed by how much the nation had improved, and it made me think of the following life lesson.

Everybody knows the Aesop fable of "The Hare and Tortoise." In my experience, the most successful people have achieved their goals through hard work and perseverance, not merely through natural talent. South Korea was a developing country when I grew up there. Through its strong work ethic and emphasis on education, it has become one of the richest countries in the world. Korea has accomplished this without any significant natural resources like oil, metals, or minerals.

Many professional head coaches or general managers started "at the bottom of the ladder" as water boys, equipment managers, or players on practice squads. The movie "Rudy" is a classic example of hard work and determination. The culmination of Rudy's dedication was the realization of his "far-fetched" goal of playing football for Notre Dame University.

All of my daughter's tennis coaches have told me that champion tennis players, either at the collegiate or professional level, have demonstrated the same personality traits. They have achieved their goals through hard work, sacrifice and self-discipline, and not because they were "born to be tennis players" or because "they won the lottery," as some people think.

There is a joke in medical school that you "see one, do one, teach one" when it comes to learning a medical or surgical procedure. The truth is that it takes practice and repetition to master a particular skill in the field of medicine. One can apply this principle to every aspect of life. Hard work will ultimately lead to long-term success.

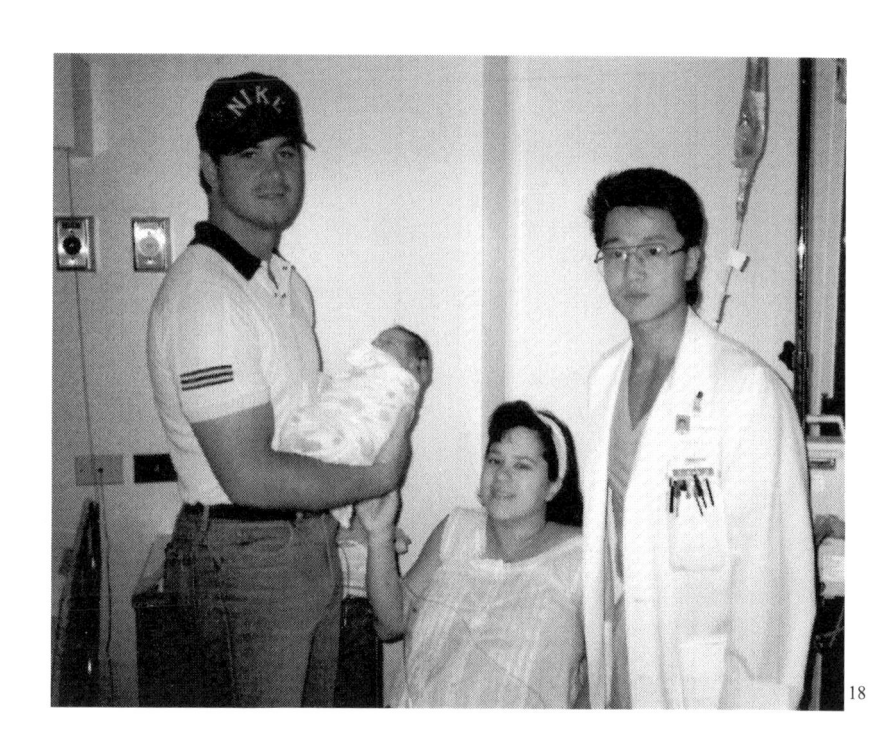

Chapter 17: Residencia Médica

My patience had finally paid off and I was now treating my own patients. After completing medical school, I decided to return to the Chicagoland area to complete my residency training in family medicine. My medical school training and experience had solidified my decision to go into the field in which I could experience continuity of care with my patients. I matched into a

---

[18] post-delivery of this baby during my family practice residency

family medicine residency program in the southwest suburbs of Chicago, near my parents' new home.

During my residency training, I treated patients of all ages from newborns to great-grandparents. To become a well rounded physician, I rotated through various specialties: pediatrics, obstetrics and gynecology, psychiatry, addiction medicine, and emergency medicine. I decided to train in emergency medicine for one month in the inner city of Chicago, at Cook County Hospital.

In the middle of one of my shifts, I saw several news reporters interviewing some of my attendings, after the premier of the TV show "ER" aired. This show is based on the experiences of physicians and patients at this hospital. The show quickly became one of my favorites, and I have seen every single episode. One of the resident physicians on the show was Ming-Na Wen. I had the privilege of chatting with her about her role on ER many years later, when we both signed autographs for fans at C2E2, the biggest comic convention in Chicago. After ER, Ming-Na played the role of Chun-Li in the movie "Street Fighter," which is based on a video game that is a rival to Mortal Kombat.

Aside from rotations outside of my main hospital, my residency training took place in Hinsdale, a rich suburb of Chicago. The majority of patients at this hospital were wealthy suburbanites. The clinic at the family practice residency, by contrast, accepted people of all economic classes. The majority of my patients were Mexican immigrants on public aid. I began speaking Spanish on a regular basis. This experience solidified my desire to practice medicine on the south side of Chicago after I graduated from residency.

During these years, I also started to lead groups on mission trips to Honduras. We traveled to villages in remote, mountainous areas of Honduras, where there was no electricity or running water. We bathed in streams or rivers, reminding me of my Korean childhood showers in the yard. We dug trenches to install water systems or build medical clinics and schools. Initially, I helped dig in the morning and then treated patients in the afternoon. The line became so long that I switched to treating patients with a nurse all day while the rest of the team dug.

Patients sometimes traveled for three days to see me, saying that I was the only doctor that they had ever seen in their lives. Hundreds of people lined up each day and I sometimes treated patients from sunrise to after sunset, when I would have to treat patients using lanterns. In spite of being isolated from "civilization," I heard a group of young men say in Spanish that they were going to ask for samples of Viagra! We did not have any, sorry!

*****

Also during residency, I was introduced to the strength and conditioning coach of the Chicago Blackhawks hockey team. He set me up with some players who wanted to take taekwondo lessons from me, and I taught each of them privately. Each player had their own *goals*, but all of them wanted to become more agile and flexible.

From working with top tier professional athletes, I have noticed that some of them are the *least* flexible taekwondo students that I have taught. I believe that at every level of athletic competition, ranging from children to professionals, flexibility and stretching are not emphasized enough. This is especially true for stretching *after* workouts and games, as part of the "cool down" process. If athletes put more emphasis on stretching and flexibility, there would be less injuries and not nearly as many athletes would end up on the "disabled list."

[19]

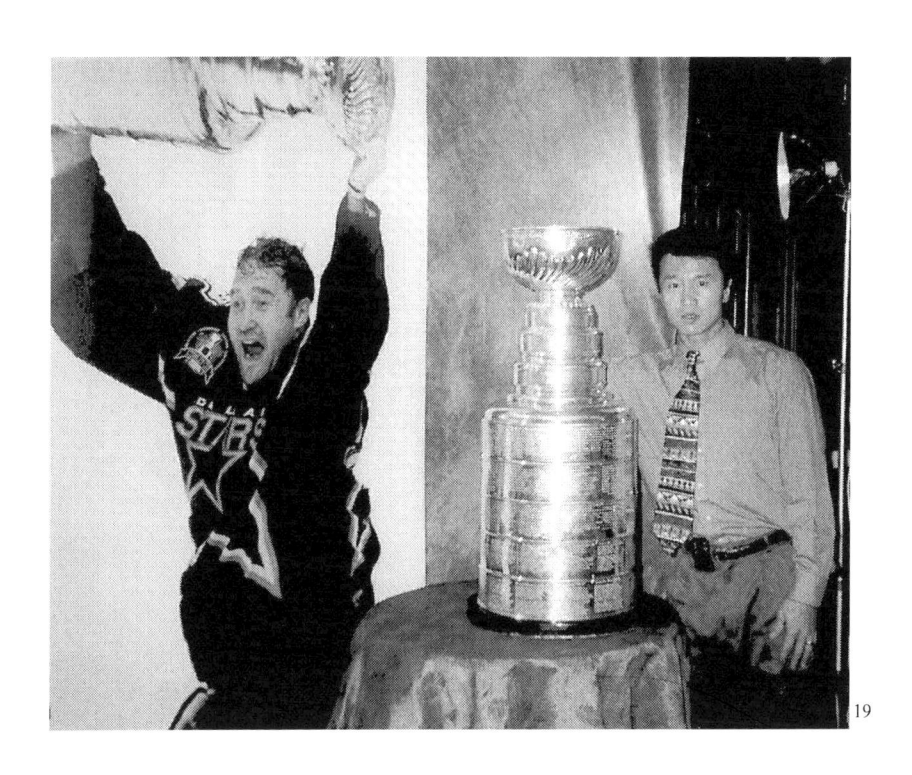

One of my Blackhawk students, Ed Belfour, went on to win the Stanley Cup with another team after leaving the Hawks. Ed had a great NHL career with several teams and was inducted into the Hockey Hall of Fame after he retired. I was honored when he invited me to his Stanley Cup party in Chicago. I mingled with several celebrity athletes, coaches and announcers, including Vladislav Tretiak, Ed's goaltending coach. Mr. Tretiak is known as

---

[19] Ed Belfour's Stanley Cup party, 1999

one of the greatest goalies to ever play hockey and was later honored to light the Olympic torch in Sochi.

During my residency I treated some celebrities, including professional athletes and their families. I once assisted in the delivery of a White Sox player's daughter, and he gave me four tickets to a Sox game. We sat right next to the Sox dugout.

At the game, a foul ball rolled toward Frank Thomas, who later became a Hall of Famer. He threw the ball toward us and my friend caught it. Two batters later, the same thing happened, and this time the ball rolled toward Bo Jackson. Bo was famous for being a great football *and* baseball player (also for his "Bo Knows" commercials for Nike). He threw us the ball, and this time, I caught it. After the game, I asked the player who gave me the tickets to have these balls autographed for us, and they did! The autographed ball from Bo is one of many precious memorabilia that I have collected throughout my life.

Even though I was busy during residency, when I was training to become a *real* doctor, I'm glad I took the time to pursue my lifelong passions, taekwondo and sports. Pursuing these diversions made my medical training more enjoyable.

[20]
Chapter 18: Mortal Kombat 2

One day during my residency years, while I was dining at a restaurant in the suburbs, I spotted a familiar face, Ho Sung Pak. We traded pleasantries and he answered my questions about his

---

[20] Filming for Shang Tsung, 1993

role in the Teenage Mutant Ninja Turtle (TMNT) movies. He further went on to say that he had recently worked as a character model for a video game that should become a hit, called Mortal Kombat (MK).

I had not played video games since high school, so I did not really fathom how popular Mortal Kombat would become. My experiences had been with early games like: Pong, Space Invaders, Asteroids and Pac Man. Toward the end of our visit, Ho Sung invited me to come to the Lakeshore Athletic Club in Chicago to train with him and other cast members of Mortal Kombat and TMNT.

Shortly after this happenchance meeting, I visited Lakeshore Athletic Club and started training with these cast members, about once a week. Even though all of them had grown up in Chicago, I had not met them before I started training with them. One character, Tony Marquez, A.K.A. Kung Lao, had even attended the same high school, Lane Tech. Because he was two years younger than me, I had not interacted with him while I was in school. He did happen to know my brother.

Most of these characters had trained in wushu or kung fu and some in karate. I was the "new kid in town" and the only one with a taekwondo background. By then I was a fifth degree black belt and these new martial arts colleagues seemed at least a little impressed by my kicks and techniques.

While training with these people, I began to notice that Mortal Kombat was indeed becoming very popular, and I saw Mortal Kombat cabinets wherever I went: arcades, movie theatres, and shopping malls. I even saw these cabinets while on vacation in Hawaii and Europe.

Soon after I began training with these martial artists, we became friends. Some even attended my wedding, years later. I remember watching the movie "Fong Sai Yuk" with them at a house party; this movie remains one of my favorites. At that party, I saw a photo that was autographed by Arnold Schwarzenegger. He wrote, "Asta la vista baby!" It was so funny to see that Arnold does not know how to spell the words to his own famous lines!

I also remember occasionally going out to clubs with my new friends, years before I took any dance classes. Because smoking was allowed inside nightclubs at that time, I did not like to frequent these establishments. I do remember running into Jeff Speakman, A.K.A., "the Perfect Weapon" and a genuinely nice guy, at one of these nightclubs.

After I trained with my new friends for a few months, I was introduced to the makers of the Mortal Kombat games, John Tobias and Ed Boon. They were impressed with my martial arts techniques. Shortly after this meeting I was asked to play a role in the sequel to Mortal Kombat.

The choices of roles I was given were either the ninjas (Scorpion, Subzero, Reptile). or Shang Tsung, who would become young to enter the tournament in Mortal Kombat 2. Since Daniel

Pesina had already played the ninjas in Mortal Kombat, I chose the role of Shang Tsung.

Yes, it is true that part of the reason why I did not want to play the ninjas was because I did not want to be covered as much as they were. Nevertheless, I do think that Daniel also offered this role to me because it was such a pain in the butt to film these characters, according to the interviews that Daniel has since given.

By the way, a number of people think or assume that I filmed for Liu Kang, because he is the stereotypical Asian character in Mortal Kombat 2. Even my cousins thought this! Sorry Ho Sung! I have even been mistaken for Phillip Rhee of the "Best of the Best" movies. Not all Asians look alike!

*****

[21]

Each of us who filmed for our individual roles as characters in Mortal Kombat 2 has his or her own story of the day we filmed. We all filmed in a small spare room in the Williams Bally Midway factory where the company makes all of its games. I was asked by

---

[21] 25 years after filming, MK2 cabinet at Galloping Ghost Arcade

Daniel Pesina and John Tobias to bring my own black martial arts pants and shoes. The rest of my costume was very cheap and flimsy. My suspenders kept falling off my shoulders while I was filming. I cannot grow much facial hair, so John drew a "Fu Manchu" goatee on my face.

Most of the moves I had to perform for the game were standard for all of the characters: low punch, high punch, low kick, high kick, block, sweep, jump, jump kick. The "flying" punches and kicks were performed on a wooden staircase. The "flips" were performed by jumping in the air and grabbing my legs; John and Ed then rotated my body via digitization to create the flip. I was not actually punched in the family jewels by Johnny Cage! I had to fake it, like I had to act like I was punched, kicked, grabbed or swept by any character. I sat on a chair and acted like I was falling into the pit.

Some of the moves and motions in Mortal Kombat 2 were my own suggestions: Shang Tsung's fighting stance is a taekwondo stance that I modified so that my body would not be covered up. My character is Chinese and thus a more traditional open handed fighting stance might have been expected. I think that my stance looks especially tough when you select me as your fighter. I do not bend my wrist in my stance or when punching or blocking, which is also from my taekwondo training. There are certain techniques where the wrist is bent in Kung Fu and other Chinese martial arts, but Shang Tsung does not use these.

Many of my high kicks were traditional taekwondo kicks and not those used in traditional Chinese martial arts. Not everyone could do a "kip-up" after falling or do a front flip and land on his back, but I could, so these techniques did not have to be computer enhanced for me.

Some of Shang Tsung's moves were the result of a collaboration between Daniel Pesina (who was a "coach" to me and other characters during filming), John Tobias, Ed Boon and myself. These include all three of my fatalities and my friendship.

Years later, with the assistance of team members of the Galloping Ghost Arcade, I uploaded these video clips "Behind the Scenes: Original Filming Footage Phillip Ahn as Shang Tsung" on my Facebook fan page so fan of Mortal Kombat 2 could see the process of creating the moves for my character.

I was able to finish all of the filming for Shang Tsung of Mortal Kombat 2 in four hours, which included getting into my costume and drawing on the goatee. John and Ed took our moves that they videotaped and digitized them to make arcade versions of Mortal Kombat 2.

Even though I had not been involved in any projects in the entertainment industry prior to filming for my role in Mortal Kombat 2, I was not nervous as I approached the day of filming. As I wrote earlier, "Some people are born great, some people achieve greatness, and some people have greatness thrust upon them." I knew that greatness would be thrust upon me as a result of filming my role in Mortal Kombat 2 and I was ready for my life to change in an exciting way.

I was one of the last characters to be filmed for Mortal Kombat 2. I remember stopping in at Midway and seeing the process of creating Mortal Kombat 2, sometimes talking to John and Ed about what moves and techniques were going to be included in the final version. The moves that were too fast or complicated, like my tornado kick, were eliminated because they were too hard to capture and digitize. A couple of moves that I thought that they should have kept were my ax kick (used in other games like Tekken) and my back handspring.

When people ask me how I feel about my role as Shang Tsung in Mortal Kombat 2, I tell them the following:

1) I was a little surprised that the characters in Mortal Kombat 2 were less realistic appearing versus the Mortal Kombat characters, especially since the graphics overall were improved.

2) I am pleased at the muscle tone definition of my character, which represented my actual level of fitness. I am also pleased how my upper cut and high side kick came out in the final version.

3) The "jump hook kick" that is in the final arcade game is not the best version that I performed on the day of filming. You can see my best such kick in the video on my fan page. I wish they had used this kick instead.

4) My character is known as a sorcerer who can morph into all of the other characters and considered by video game magazines as one of the most powerful fighting characters. While this is cool, I would like to have had something unique to my character, like Sub Zero's ability to freeze people, Scorpion's "Get over here" spear throw, the "nut punch" by Johnny Cage and the "bicycle kick" by Liu Kang.

5) Liu Kang performs a dance for his "Friendship." This would have been more fitting for me, as you will read later.

6) I was very happy to see that my "Fatalities" were not anything that could be copycatted, even by the mentally unstable.

Sorry to disappoint my fans, but I have yet to be able to perform any of my Fatalities, Friendships or Babalities while playing my own game, *and*, I have lost several times to young gamers, even when they have used me as their fighter!

Overall, I thought that Mortal Kombat 2 was a great finished product and I knew that it would be a huge hit with fans. Of course, at that time, I had no idea that it would still be popular with fans decades later. It is at least a little surprising that Mortal Kombat 2 has remained the favorite version from the entire Mortal Kombat series for a large percentage of fans.

LIFE LESSON: Work hard and develop skills that are desirable to others. You will then be ready when you are given the opportunity to display these skills.

PHILLIP AHN M.D.
AS
SHANG TSUNG

Chapter 19: Moral Kombat

I am a Christian who believes in living according to principles. I try to follow the Bible verse that says, "Whatever you do, work at it with all your heart, as working for God, not for men." This includes being able to explain and having good reasons for making

---

[22] My credits at the end of the game, Mortal Kombat 2

decisions for doing what I do. Before I accepted my role as Shang Tsung in Mortal Kombat 2, I performed a literature search (Google was several years from being invented) on "the effect of video game violence on societal behavior."

There was limited literature on video game violence at that time, but the overall conclusion that was drawn was that the closer to reality that something is, the more likely it can be copycatted by participants. Mortal Kombat, like all fighting games, can be reproduced by its players, in terms of punching and kicking. The more graphic scenarios cannot be reproduced: pulling out one's heart or spine, sawing a person in half with a hat, or stealing souls.

The video games that have been successfully copycatted, albeit by people who were mentally unstable, have been shooting games, such as Doom. Even these games have had some positive effect on society: people who grew up playing such games have gone on to become great soldiers and fighter pilots.

In the big picture, people have to remember that Mortal Kombat 2 is a game, created for entertainment, like movies and sporting events. An example of how Mortal Kombat 2 falls into the entertainment category is that players can perform "Friendships" and "Babalities", not just "Fatalities," on their opponents.

Martial arts can be used for good like self-defense or protecting another person, and for self-discipline. But it can be used for evil, if either the practitioner or the instructor has bad intentions, like the villains who used it for bullying in the movie "Karate Kid."

I imagined being given the opportunity to become a professional boxer like Manny Pacquiao, a mixed martial artist like Matt Hughes or a hockey player like Jerome Iginla. Being in these roles *may* mean that I have to hurt or knock out my opponent, and it *may* potentially incite violent tendencies in other people and lead to copycat behavior. Keeping all of this in mind, I asked myself if I would be okay with my decision to participate in these opportunities. The answer was "Yes!" Thus, I accepted my role to become Shang Tsung in Mortal Kombat 2. I was reminded of Martin Luther's quote, "Love God and sin boldly."

Professional athletes, martial artists, or movie stars can use their popularity to inspire positive behavior in others, especially the youth. I wholeheartedly believed that I could do the same with my inevitable "role model" opportunity as a video game character.

Shortly after filming for my role in Mortal Kombat 2, I received a call from an agent who was looking for martial artists to film a beer commercial. I declined, explaining my desire to be a positive influence, and told her that I also would not participate in any filming that promoted smoking, using illegal drugs, or explicit nudity. I was not (and am not), by any means, legalistic or puritanical, but I did not want to be perceived by the public, especially my young fans, as promoting behaviors or attitudes that could be harmful if practiced.

LIFE LESSON: You can't please everybody, so don't try. Do what you believe is right in every situation, give everything your wholehearted effort, and don't worry about the results. Stand up for your principles, but back it up with sound reasoning or evidence, not feelings or emotions. As Paul says in the Bible, "Always be prepared to give the reason for the hope that you have. But do this with gentleness and respect." Then "let go and let God," as I have previously written.

Mortal Kombat is symbolic of life, where you have teammates, as well as opponents. You will always have critics, but everybody does. Jesus Christ Himself had "haters" against him. Paul tells Timothy that, "Everyone who wants to live a godly life will be persecuted." And, unfortunately, your critics usually are louder than your supporters, which is an unfortunate fact of life. I plead for my fans and readers to help reverse this trend. I would love to see more people praise and credit someone when they see good work or good deeds, criticize less when others make mistakes, and "put yourself in their shoes".

Chapter 20: Fame Without Fortune

A couple of months after my filming, all of the characters came to a photoshoot to create the promotional flier for Mortal Kombat 2. This flier was later used as the cover for a gaming magazine. Soon after this, a gaming magazine editor came to the gym and interviewed each of us, giving each character a full page

---

[23] Photoshoot for the new MK2 characters, 1993

154

biography. A couple of details in my biography are wrong, which readers can figure out using the stories of this book.

I eagerly anticipated the release of Mortal Kombat 2 into arcades. When this happened, I inconspicuously went to watch people play, without revealing myself as a character. Even to this day, I have probably been recognized only a handful of times in the general public, and that is because fans have seen how I look on social media. As I have stated earlier, I have been mistaken for Liu Kang numerous times, and even Kung Lao, although rarely.

From 1993 to around 1996, I enjoyed newfound fame and popularity. Some would say notoriety since Mortal Kombat 2 was a bit controversial because of its graphic violence. Being a character in a world famous video game, that people related to like they do movie stars, turned my life around. I was "morphed" from a shy, insecure boy to a confident, sought after young man.

Fans stood in long lines at martial arts tournaments, video game stores and conventions, to get autographs from this once pathologically shy boy. I believe that I was ready for this new found fame and popularity at this point in my life. I had dreamed of being a professional athlete or martial artist when I was growing up. I dreamed of being popular (versus the shy, insecure kid that I was), but also a positive role model.

When I signed autographs and replied to fan mail, I tried to be a positive influence, especially to the young and impressionable. I remember how young people loved dancing with me at post-tournament parties and how I felt like one of the popular kids that I looked up to when I was young.

At the height of our popularity, I remember that my fellow Mortal Kombat 2 characters and I had hundreds of autograph seekers at martial arts tournaments. At one tournament, a father and son martial artist acting duo was inducted into the organization's Hall of Fame. This duo had a short line of autograph seekers at their booth, while the line at our booth was *much* longer.

Another memory is that at a junior national taekwondo tournament, we signed autographs until midnight.

Besides signing autographs for fans, I filmed a couple of commercials for local arcades and video game stores and martial arts catalogs. One such catalog that I was asked to appear in was that of Asian World of Martial Arts (AWMA). When I was approached for this project by its owners, I told them that they should also talk to Daniel Pesina (Johnny Cage and the ninjas in Mortal Kombat and Mortal Kombat 2) about this as well. He was photographed for this catalog, but I was not asked again. I think that there was miscommunication and that AWMA thought that I was not interested. Oh well, I am glad Daniel did get in their catalog, especially since he helped me get my part as Shang Tsung.

Another memory I have is when we, the characters from Mortal Kombat 2, participated in a martial arts demonstration at Lakeshore Athletic Club with Danny Bonaduce, who had some martial arts training. Prior to this day his fame had faded since his glory days as Danny Partridge of the Partridge Family band TV show. I believe that doing a demonstration with us was a small stepping stone in re-establishing his status as a celebrity. Shortly after this demonstration, Danny participated in a celebrated boxing match against Donnie Osmond, a famous singer and entertainer. I wish that Danny had challenged me instead!

    I also remember being asked by a pharmaceutical company to be the keynote speaker for a regional meeting of their pharmaceutical representatives. I gave a short taekwondo demonstration, and then told them my life story. The company made two life sized photos, one of me performing a sidekick and one of me as a physician, which they used to promote the event. The pharmaceutical representative who invited me for the event told me afterwards that she was impressed and found me to be a truly unique speaker.

    For several years, I gave interviews for other magazines and radio shows, and spoke at venues like elementary and martial arts schools. I felt honored, humbled, and thankful to God that I was given such opportunities. It felt like a dream come true, that it happened to a kid who was shy and insecure and looked up to exactly the type of person that I had become.

About a year after filming together, some fellow Mortal Kombat 2 actors and I were invited by Atari Jaguar to film for a new video game. The company wanted to release this game to make a comeback in the video game industry. We were flown to the Electronic Entertainment Expo (E3) in Los Angeles to promote this game.

While at the expo, I mingled with some of the characters of Mortal Kombat 3, as well as other celebrities. This included former Olympic gymnast Dominique Dawes, former NFL great Ronnie Lott and MLB legend Orlando Cepeda, and one of my favorite music groups, Earth, Wind and Fire. Unfortunately, the reviews of this game by fans were not good, and the game "Thea Realm Fighters" was never released.

A fun memory I have of this trip is when I joked around with Daniel Pesina (as I often do) and created mock Mortal Kombat characters for "Mad" Magazine. I never shared my creations with the magazine, but these are some of the best ideas that made Daniel laugh all night:

1. "Roo Kang," whose "bicycle kick" is that of a kangaroo kicking while laying back on his tail, and a joey popping out of the kangaroo's pouch to throw a low fireball.
2. "Kung Pao," a chicken who throws his comb instead of a hat.
3. "Frigidaire, " a refrigerator version of Sub Zero who throws ice cubes and blows cold air.
4. "Gordo," a fat version of Goro.

Soon after filming for Thea Realm Fighters, the brother-in-law of Ho Sung Pak filmed the same people for a video game that he wanted to produce. By this time, I had become a video game "veteran" and I was able to film my character "Kyu," my original Korean middle name, in an hour and a half. Again, unfortunately, this game was never released.

Ho Sung Pak filmed trailers for a couple of movies after filming for Mortal Kombat and Mortal Kombat 2. One of these movies was going to be titled, "A Common Enemy." Many of the characters in Mortal Kombat 2, including me, filmed some fight scenes for this movie, but it never made it to theaters.

Because of the organizational skills I had developed, I was able to participate in filming, interviews, commercials, and public speaking, while also leading medical mission trips and completing my family medicine residency in three years, without any interruptions.

*****

Fame can change people and it changed me in a positive way. Sometimes, fame changes the person who becomes the "celebrity", but also changes his or her "friends." When I attended the wedding of friends from my medical school years, some guests treated me differently than they had before I filmed for Mortal Kombat 2. More than one woman made suggestive comments towards me, even though I brought a date to the wedding. One asked me to dance with her and said afterwards, "You can be my doctor any day." Wow! I did not see that coming.

Later in my medical career, I had similar reactions from some female patients that did not even know of my "celebrity" status in Mortal Kombat 2. There was a young woman who repeatedly had mildly high blood pressure and heart rate. After her third such visit I said to her, "I can't understand why a healthy young woman like you would have high blood pressure and heart rate." She candidly said to me, "To be honest, I have never had a male doctor. And, to be honest, I've never had a young male doctor. *And*, to be honest, I've never had an attractive, young male doctor." I was flattered.

On another occasion, another female patient confessed to me, "I've been having inappropriate thoughts…about my doctor!"

I was both flattered and a little scared, but I calmly treated her like all of my other patients. These stories may seem like bragging, and they are, but to me these moments reminded me of how far I had come from being a shy and bullied outsider. Through hard work and confronting my obstacles, I had morphed from being an insecure adolescent to an "attractive" and accomplished physician.

*****

For my role in developing my character as Shang Tsung, I was paid a one day modeling fee. Mortal Kombat 2, like Mortal Kombat, became very popular, so that the makers of the game at Midway entered into contracts to make Mortal Kombat 2 console games for Sega Genesis and Nintendo, toys, action figures, movies, and more. Most fans with whom I've had conversations or interviews assume that we, the original characters of Mortal Kombat and Mortal Kombat 2, have received royalties from these projects.

Midway's representatives and attorneys met with all of the Mortal Kombat and Mortal Kombat 2 characters to try to get us to sign away the rights to earn royalties or residuals from any projects related to these games. A few of us signed, but some characters did not. I was willing to go along with the majority, and we did not sign this contract but instead filed a lawsuit.

Unfortunately, the judge in our case threw our lawsuit out of court without any judgement against Midway. Of course, filing the lawsuit precluded the other characters and me from being invited to participate in Mortal Kombat 3 and future Mortal Kombat projects. In spite of this outcome, I definitely believe that everything happens for a reason, according to God's providence, and I try not to live with any regrets.

I am very loyal to my friends and family, employer and in general whoever enters my life and develops a close relationship with me. I was very grateful to my fellow Mortal Kombat characters, for allowing me to work out with them and subsequently asking me to be part of the Mortal Kombat franchise as Shang Tsung.

LIFE LESSON: God is in control. I do not believe in luck and I never wish anyone "good luck." As the wise Grand Master Oogway from "Kung Fu Panda" said, "There are no accidents." Everything happens for a reason, reasons that sometimes we can't understand with human minds. "Let go and let God." Don't let your past define you or determine your future. "Adversity builds character." Admit and learn from your mistakes, "live and learn", but don't live with regrets. "Be anxious for nothing." "Don't sweat the small stuff." What is small stuff, you ask? "Everything is small stuff!"

Chapter 21: Ahn's Academy of Taekwondo

Shortly after I began my medical practice, I used my free-time to open a taekwondo school with my brother. We kept the same name and logo as that of my father's schools in Chicago, where we received our training as adolescents.

---

[24] The Illinois USTU taekwondo team coaches, circa 2000

166

I also resumed instructing the Wheaton College Taekwondo Club that I founded when I was a sophomore at Wheaton College. The club had continued for over ten consecutive years, under the instruction of my brother and his assistant instructors, who were my first students when I started the club.

Like myself, my brother taught taekwondo as a hobby. He graduated from Wheaton College with a business degree, received his MBA from the University of Chicago, and subsequently received his PhD and became a professor of Business Economics. He is a year and a half younger than me and we definitely developed some "sibling rivalry" when we were children. Growing up, we were usually captains of opposing teams during pickup football or basketball games. Overall, his characteristics align more with my father, while I am more like my mother.

Part of what makes the martial artist community so enjoyable is how diverse it can be and the various successes of former taekwondo students. For example, two of my students and eventual assistant instructors were Camille and Kennerly, the "Harp Twins", who are now very popular harpists and YouTube sensations and have performed at similar events to which other Mortal Kombat 2 characters and I have been invited.

In the early 2000's, I became the chairman of the taekwondo competition of the Prairie State Games. Prairie State Games is an Olympic style of competition with a variety of sports in which one initially competes against athletes in his or her own state, Illinois, and then advances to compete against the winners in other states.

Because I had developed organizational skills, and with the assistance of the other black belts, I was able to start and finish this annual tournament in about four hours, even though we had hundreds of competitors. This is in contrast to normal taekwondo tournaments, which are notorious for starting late and running late, sometimes well into the evening.

I also met professional athletes at the regional competitions, including one of the top Olympic track stars in history, Jackie Joyner-Kersee.

I was also invited to be one of the coaches for the Illinois USTU taekwondo team, which would send the winners to the national tournament and then the Olympic trials, during Olympic years. Some of my own students from my school were on the Illinois team and I coached them at the national tournament that year. It was a great experience and honor, even though they did not become national medalists.

Most of my duties consisted of conditioning, and I had the athletes jog two miles with me, while doing 50 – 100 yard sprints several times during the run. Even though I was their trainer, all but one of the athletes soon fell way behind me; the one that kept up with me was a former female collegiate soccer player. I got the same results when I trained other national champions on other occasions.

I am proud to say that my daughter adopted this training exercise, incorporating sprints while jogging, into her regular training regimen after I made her do this with me when she was around eight years old. She did not enjoy it back then, but during high school, she was the one who initiated this exercise and made me do it with her!

On other occasions, I accompanied some students to coach them at the Olympic trials at the Olympic Training Center in Colorado Springs. Even though they did not ultimately make the Olympic team, it was an incredible experience, especially because I was able to see and interact with eventual Olympic medalists.

My father operated his taekwondo schools without forcing his students to sign long contracts, and my brother and I did the same. Almost all other martial arts schools (and health clubs) do have students sign contracts obligating them to make long term payments, whether they attend classes or not.

Because my brother and I did not want to resort to this business practice, our school became a financial burden rather than a blessing. We eventually decided not to renew our lease and closed our school. We moved on and still enjoyed teaching as part-time staff members at health clubs and other taekwondo schools.

I am a busy family physician, but I have practiced martial arts much longer than I have practiced medicine. Being able to continue my family's tradition of sharing the art of taekwondo has been a rewarding experience and essential in shaping who I am today. Both of these fields require discipline, and I have been able to apply the self discipline that I have learned in martial arts to studying and practicing medicine.

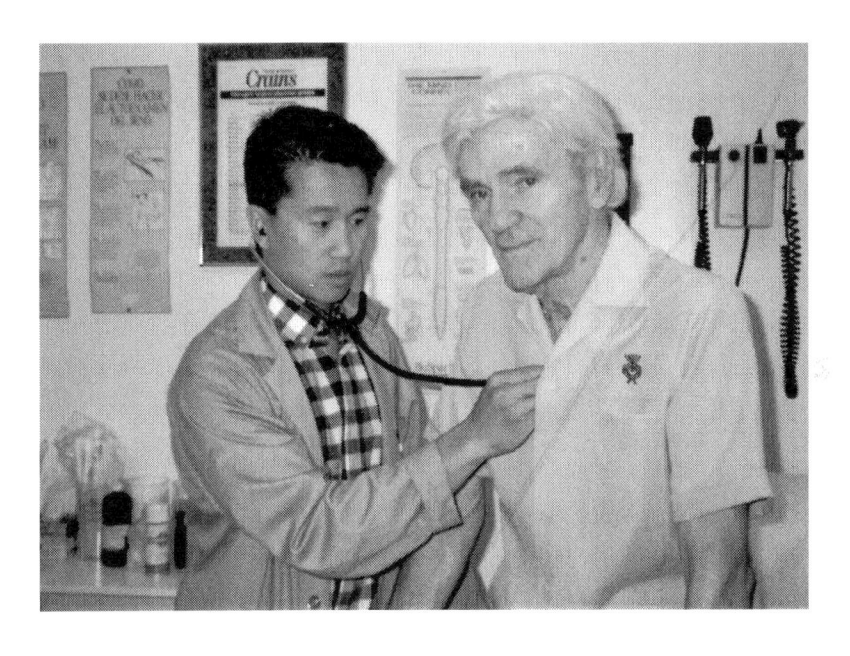

Chapter 22: Práctica Médica

After completing my family medicine residency, I began my medical practice, in clinics for a hospital system on the south side of Chicago. I have worked in this area for my entire medical career, and a majority of my patients are low to middle income class minorities, predominantly Latin Americans.

I take pride in being the busiest employed physician at my hospital, sometimes treating over 40 patients per day. This is partly because I accept "walk-ins" for sick or injured patients, while other offices don't. I am also busy because I am flexible (not just in martial arts) about patients being late, if they have a legitimate excuse. Of course, I am also busy because my patients are loyal to me.

Everyone thinks that they are original when they call me "Dr. Phil" (some physicians even call me this). One of my patients thought that my name was "Dr. Oz" and called me by this name at every visit.

As a family practitioner, I treat patients from the cradle to the grave. My practice consists of several roles: pediatrician, gynecologist, dermatologist, minor surgeon, internist and even, psychiatrist. Every aspect of my job is rewarding, albeit sometimes exhausting.

I have found that a large percent of physical symptoms are caused by psychological issues, including anxiety, depression, or "adjustment disorder." The last diagnosis relates to how one reacts poorly to stressful events in his or her life, not on a chronic basis like the other two conditions. All of these psychological issues can arise from low self-esteem or cause feelings of low self-worth.

I give my patients the following advice when it comes to handling stress:

1)"Breathe."

2) "Count your blessings."

3) "See the big picture."

4) "Let go and let God."

Life can be cyclical. You can either be in a vicious cycle or a virtuous cycle.

Vicious Cycle

- poor self-esteem (self-pity)
- poor performance
- poor self-discipline
- poor work ethic (apathy)

Virtuous Cycle

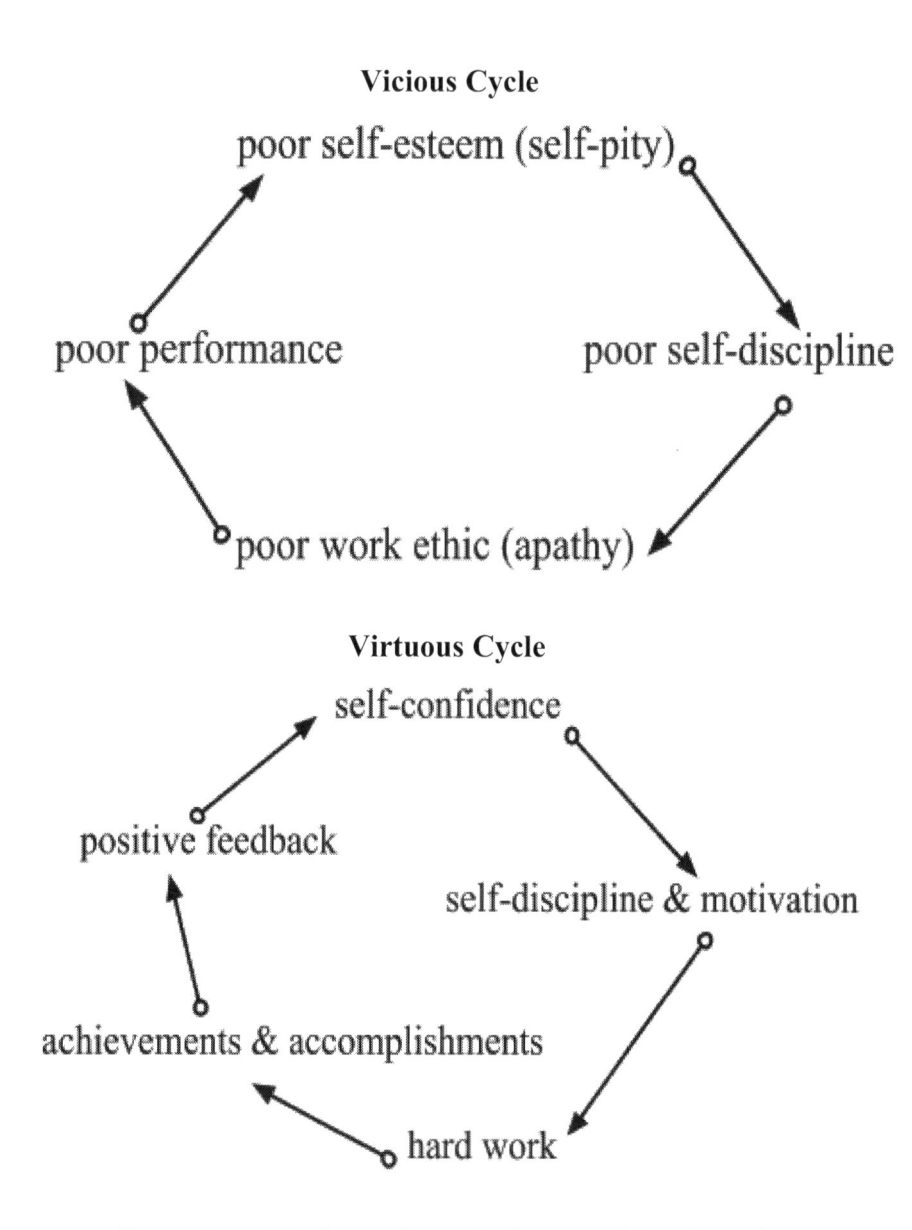

- self-confidence
- positive feedback
- self-discipline & motivation
- achievements & accomplishments
- hard work

There is no "fool proof" method to transition from the vicious cycle to the virtuous cycle. The recommended strategy is to start one thing, like exercise, that may be the domino you need to knock down the rest, to start the process of metamorphosis ("morphing").

I tell all of my patients to exercise, to "just do it." You will be successful if you "start low and go slow." Break up your routine if necessary and do several small workouts throughout the day. If you don't have the time, you don't have to exercise for an hour because "Something is better than nothing." If you don't feel like exercising, still "go through the motions" when tempted to skip a workout. I have discovered that this can provide you with unexpected energy to finish your workout or to accomplish more than you had anticipated. Also, keep trying until you find an activity that you enjoy. It can be running, cycling, swimming, weight lifting, Zumba, dancing, playing sports or doing martial arts. Exercise will give you the motivation you need to become productive, which will improve your self-esteem.

I once attended a sports medicine conference in Kona, Hawaii. One of the perks of being a physician has been attending conferences in exotic places, including the Bahamas, the Cayman Islands, the Hawaiian islands, Cabo San Lucas, Puerto Rico, and various cruises.

Those that attended the conference in Kona were able to volunteer for that year's Iron Man competition (2.4 miles swimming, 112 miles cycling and 26.2 miles running). While I did not have to do much during the race, providing the occasional athlete with intravenous fluids, I enjoyed participating in all of the festivities. I especially enjoyed the "carb loading" meal on the eve of the race.

By volunteering, I received some Iron Man paraphernalia, including some shirts and tank tops. When people have noticed the Iron Man shirts, they have asked me or even assumed that I competed in the Iron Man. I laugh and say, "I only have fast twitch fibers; my triathlon would consist of the 50 meter (one lap) swim, the 100 meter dash, and the long jump."

Having feasted with these athletes on the eve of the race reminds me of another advice that I give my patients. "Carbs are not your enemy!" I do not advocate any extreme diets like the Atkins or Keto diets. Don't equate "sweets" with carbs and don't equate "sugar" with type 2 diabetes. There are good and bad carbs, so choose wisely. Good carbs are what you need to use as fuel for exercise, which is the key to a healthy body and mind.

I try to do what is best for my patient in every situation. For example, I do not prescribe antibiotics for common colds. I rarely prescribe controlled substances and the word has spread "in the streets" so I am not frequented by drug seeking patients. I "tell it like it is" and don't "beat around the bush" and don't tell patients what they want to hear. "Honesty is (normally) the best policy." Billy Joel sings, "Honesty is such a lonely word, hardly ever heard, and mostly what I need from you."

Most patients appreciate my candid nature and often say that I am the only doctor that has ever been straightforward. Some patients drive over 30 miles to see me, after they have moved out of the neighborhood. Yes, I do lose some patients because they don't get what they want, but I have to live and practice by my principles.

Both of my parents have long outlived their parents because of the care they have received from their physician – me! To their credit, they have become very compliant patients. They have changed their diet and exercise regimen after I diagnosed them developing chronic medical problems.

Doctor visits can be a very vulnerable experience and it is important that my patients are comfortable with me. One example is when a patient came to me complaining of a foul vaginal odor for one month. My nurse and I examined her and I pulled out a black foreign object. I asked her, "What is this?" She was embarrassed when she replied, in Spanish, "My husband and I are separated, but he came over one night, was drunk, and wanted [intimacy]. We didn't have [protection], so we used sandwich bags." Unfortunately, she had left a couple of bags inside, for a month! I treated her and reassured her that she would be fine. She was grateful.

A male patient said to me, nonchalantly, in Spanish, "What would happen if my girlfriend snorted cocaine from my [private part]?" This brazen question startled me for a second, but then I scolded him, in Spanish. Cocaine destroys blood vessels. It is bad enough that he is risking damage to his nasal passages, heart and brain. Did he want to damage the vessels in his private part? I hope he heeded my warning.

Besides being honest and straightforward, I try to "inject" humor into my visits with my patients. "Laughter is the best medicine." While this phrase is not absolutely true, it's a good guideline. I tell my patients and friends to try to enjoy life and not to complain. It is not pleasant being around chronic complainers, so don't become one. Develop a sense of humor. Become witty. Crack jokes! Try not to be so sensitive and learn to laugh at yourself. I've learned throughout my life that women are usually attracted to fun guys that make them laugh.

*****

I am very blessed to have experienced very few patient deaths while they were under my care. Two young adolescents were shot by gang members. One child died from cancer. A young mother also succumbed to cancer, while another young mom died from meningitis. Yes, I have lost other patients throughout the years, but they were elderly, from natural causes.

I did experience one particular tragedy involving a young man. One day, I received a call from my brother that one of our former black belts, who was then a college student, had died. I knew that the cause must have been either a congenital heart defect, which prematurely kills some athletes, or a drug overdose. I was hoping that it was not the latter, but it was. This young man died of a heroin overdose. I had taught him from the age of eight, along with his father and sister. He was a quiet kid who seemed to have his life together in terms of academics and martial arts. I attended his funeral and tried to help comfort his family.

Please don't use drugs. Do not give into peer pressure. Find other, positive ways to deal with pain and stress. I have listed several better coping methods throughout the book, like exercise and finding healthy hobbies. Seek professional help if these methods do not resolve your pain or suffering.

Studying to become a physician and working as one can be very demanding. It can also be very rewarding and fulfilling, if you enter the field of medicine and your speciality with the right motives. Aside from working in Chicago, I have used my skills as a physician to lead groups on numerous mission trips to Honduras, Haiti and Jamaica. I feel very blessed that God has given me these opportunities to provide medical care to the disadvantaged in Chicago and overseas.

[25]

Chapter 23: Life Goes On

Three years after graduating from my family medicine residency, finally practicing medicine in Chicago and starting my taekwondo school, I married Danielle. We met at a church sponsored dance party in the suburbs of Chicago and married after two years of dating.

---

[25] Safely in the bull ring after running with the bulls in Pamplona, Spain, 1999

I did not know that I had played basketball with her brothers prior to meeting her. The running joke was that I asked one of her brothers, who stands 6 feet 3 inches tall, if he had a sister, because I wanted a professional athlete for a child. I do not remember saying this.

Danielle was in law school at the time we met. I drove her to and from the train station to attend school in Chicago and we listened to tapes on the topics that she had to study for her bar exam. I knew Criminal Procedure at least as well as she did, from having watched the TV show "Law and Order." Even though I played a villain in Mortal Kombat 2, I would have made a great prosecuting attorney!

Years later, when we were involved in a lawsuit in small claims court over property matters, I was cool and collected, even using legal jargon like, "Objection!" when the plaintiffs made an illegitimate charge. Danielle, by contrast, was very anxious, having prepared for several hours before the trial. The plaintiffs also appeared very nervous, especially when the judge agreed with my objection. The judge ruled that Danielle and I, the defendants, did nothing wrong. Our realtor did have to pay the plaintiffs some money for his misrepresentation of the property.

Danielle passed her bar exam and soon began practicing as an attorney. We enjoyed a comfortable suburban life, working and traveling regularly. We did not have a "white picket fence" nor did we care to "keep up with the Joneses," but there was nothing that I felt that we lacked.

During one of our vacations, I ran with the bulls in Pamplona, Spain, which I dreamed of doing since I was in college. I read Ernest Hemingway's "The Sun Also Rises" on my way to Pamplona; this book supposedly popularized the annual "San Fermin" festival.

I watched ESPN's annual taping of this event, so I became very familiar with the course that I would run. I knew to avoid the "Hamburger Wall," where a runner becomes hamburger if he gets caught between a bull and the wall, and learned some "golden rules." One golden rule was, "If you go down, you stay down," until you *know* that all of the bulls have passed.

There has been one American "fatality" in the entire history of this fest, and it was precisely because the runner violated this golden rule. He was gored to death when he got up after falling. Ironically, he was from the suburbs of Chicago, and he was going to start medical school after returning from his trip. I was interviewed by ESPN after I completed my run and made it to the bull ring.

On another vacation, I Greek line danced with Supreme Court Justice Ruth Bader Ginsburg, who was a guest lecturer in Crete, where Danielle studied that summer. Judge Ginsburg told Danielle, "Your husband is a great dancer!"

*****

Shortly after my daughter was born, America suffered one of the biggest tragedies in its history. This event became constantly televised for several weeks and it affected every aspect of society all over the world, especially in the United States. The event that I'm describing is "9-11," when terrorists flew airplanes into the twin towers of the World Trade Center, on September 11, 2001. Many people died and countless' lives were negatively affected by these acts of terror, but many heroes emerged from this event as well. Their stories have shaped my perspective of heroism.

Two of those heroes that I want to mention are Pat Tillman and Todd Beamer. Tillman was an NFL football player who had just signed a contract for around $10 million and had also recently married. When 9-11 happened, he sacrificed all of this and joined the army to become an army ranger, in the hopes of catching the people who were responsible for committing the above act of terror. Unfortunately and tragically, he was killed by friendly fire two years later.

Todd Beamer was on another flight that fateful morning. He learned that his plane was going to be used in another act of terror, after the first plane had flown into the twin towers. We would later learn that the terrorists had planned to fly this plane into the Pentagon in Washington D.C. Todd rounded up other men to stop these terrorists and shouted, "Let's roll." These men sacrificed their lives as the plane crash landed in a field instead of its original target.

Todd was a graduate of Wheaton College, my alma mater, although he attended after I had already graduated. His wife Lisa also attended Wheaton College with Todd. She later wrote the best-selling book "Let's Roll," in which she recounts that fateful day, as well as the days that led up to and followed this day in history. I have imagined doing the same things as Pat Tillman and Todd Beamer did if I were in their situations. They will always be two of my heroes.

LIFE LESSON: Live life to the fullest, with a purpose. Be a hero everyday, to your family, friends, coworkers, patients, or even to strangers.

Chapter 24: Parenthood

Danielle and I were blessed by God with a daughter, three years after we married. We named her "Abygale" from the Biblical name "Abigail," which means "father's joy" or "joy of the father." She is described in the Bible as "good in discretion and beautiful in form."

---

[26] "Bring your daughter to work," 2001

I try not to follow trends or being like everyone else, so I avoid trendy clothes or cars. This avoidance extends to trendy grammatical errors, like "this is a photo of John and I" or "he is REAL good at swimming." Thus, I was very relieved when Danielle and I decided to give our daughter a unique spelling of her name. The name "Abigail" soon became popular after her birth.

After my daughter was born, I became a doting dad: feeding my daughter, changing her diapers, and even taking her on late night walks in a "Baby Bjorn" carrier to calm her down when she cried. Danielle decided to return to work when Abygale was three months old, so I sometimes finished seeing patients while carrying her in the Baby Bjorn. One day, I was walking around the neighborhood of my clinic during lunch time with my daughter in her carrier. A female patient noticed this and expressed her admiration for me by saying, "My husband won't even think to change our children's diapers." Fathers, remember that parenthood means sharing the responsibilities of raising a child.

I spent most of my free time with Abygale, and she eventually became a beautiful, smart, and athletic child. Because of her, I was able to live my first American childhood, since my first eight years of life were spent in Korea. Together, we watched "Snow White," "Beauty and the Beast," "Cinderella," "Pinocchio," "Bambi" and other classics, which marked the first time for both of us. I did not realize that Bambi, short for Bambino, was a male! Why is it such a popular name for female strippers?

Danielle and I taught Abygale how to read, swim and play sports. At four years of age, after watching me teach taekwondo for one year, she expressed a desire to participate in classes. I usually recommend that children start classes at around age six, so I thought that Abygale would endure a few classes before she became bored. Four years later, she tested for and received her first degree black belt.

One of my fondest memories of my daughter's childhood is attending father–daughter dances together. Before the first such dance, the DJ asked each father if he wanted to dedicate a song to his daughter. I chose the song, "Sweet Child of Mine" by Guns N' Roses. Even though it is not a great song to dance to, the dads and volunteering moms loved it when the DJ played it because it is not a common choice. My daughter and I look back at this event whenever we hear this song.

LIFE LESSON: A father's relationship with his daughter or son is often the most important thing in the child's life. Treat your daughter like a princess (not a diva), as you want her future husband to treat her. If you don't do this, she will look for such affirmation elsewhere, and this can lead to bad situations such as promiscuity, domestic abuse, drug abuse or even prostitution. Fathers also need to be involved with and be role models for their sons. This will produce future gentlemen, who are respectful, faithful and confident, who will be great husbands and fathers themselves.

*****

When my daughter was born, my athletic dreams evolved from becoming a professional athlete to being the father of one. While she was enrolled in taekwondo classes, I introduced Abygale to tennis, initially once a week at a local park district.

---

[27] My daughter could beat me in tennis by age 12

She also participated in swimming, diving, and some gymnastics. Because she started diving at age five, including going off the high dive, I started to perform flips and tricks off the diving board as well. Prior to this, I had not been on a diving board since high school! I also taught my daughter how to snorkel, when we were on vacation in Hawaii. Knowing how to swim may have saved Abygale's life in Costa Rica. When she was six, we were caught in a riptide and I told her to swim with the current until it calms down and allows us to swim ashore. She did, and was not fazed, until I told her that we had just survived a riptide!

Not only did we bond over playing sports together, but I wanted to support my daughter in her passions. Abygale became more and more proficient in tennis, so I gradually placed her in more frequent and advanced levels of instruction. She eventually won enough matches and tournaments to become one of the top ten players in Chicago and the Midwest by age twelve.

In junior high school, Abygale became interested in volleyball. I was a dedicated father and tried to be a coach and trainer to her in all of her sports. I volunteered to be an assistant coach for her club volleyball team in 7th grade. The teams were named for their uniforms' colors, and ours was Navy. I sometimes played the song, "In the Navy" by the Village People for my team when we practiced.

I tried to bring out the best for each team member and gave practical advice like, "Remember 'high and middle' when serving, especially during stressful situations when the game is on the line". After one of our wins in which one of our players served 10 straight aces to mount a comeback, she told me, "I kept telling myself, 'High, Middle'." Our team went undefeated and did not even lose a set going into the championship match.

Unfortunately, we lost a very close three set match, after having match (and championship) point. We had a comfortable lead and decided to play one of our weaker players. After several mistakes, the opposing team gained confidence, the momentum turned and they beat us. Our team's scenario reminded me of the 2007 New England Patriots football team, who had a perfect 16 – 0 record and were heavily favored to win the Super Bowl, but lost to the New York Giants 17 – 14. As you can imagine, my team members were crushed. I took several of them out for pizza afterwards, as consolation.

LIFE LESSON: Be a gracious winner and not a sore loser. Also, be a good sport overall. While winning is fun, try to enjoy the journey.

I can't stand trash talkers. While trash talking is sometimes funny and can distract opponents or make them play poorly, it often backfires and instead gives opponents motivation.

All athletes " don't feel it" on certain days. My daughter's friend was having one of those days during a tennis match and her opponent, having match point, was celebrating her "inevitable" win. This opponent made the mistake of taunting my daughter's friend, and this fueled her to mount an incredible comeback and win her match! Classy winners, as well as classy losers, are respected by fans.

******

I considered myself a "loving disciplinarian." Through trial and error, I have learned that a majority of people, especially children, are motivated by positive reinforcement. You should be honest with them so that they can improve and learn from mistakes, but it is extremely important to reinforce their strengths and positive traits.

I was very wary of becoming an overbearing father-coach, but I will be the first to admit that I did make this mistake at times. There are many examples of parents taking their coaching too far. My daughter and I watched ESPN's "30 for 30" special on Todd and Marv Marinovich.

Marv controlled every aspect of Todd's life as soon as he was born; technically, his controlling started when his ex-wife was pregnant with Todd. Todd was placed on a strict diet and exercise program because Marv's dream was to groom his son to become an NFL quarterback. Todd did not even taste ice cream until he was on his own in college. Away from his father, he also tried marijuana; maybe he ate ice cream because he "got the munchies." Marv's over-controlling and micromanaging of Todd briefly allowed Todd to become an NFL quarterback. Ultimately, Todd rebelled against his strict upbringing and began to progressively use more and harder drugs. This spiral of abuse caused him to prematurely drop out of football.

Bad sportsmanship does not only apply to athletes. Abygale and I also watched the "30 for 30" special on the Cubs fans' mistreatment and bullying of a fellow loyal fan, Steve Bartman. Other Cubs fans blamed this mild mannered young man for the Cubs losing a playoff game and not making it to the World Series. They threw beer and garbage at him as he was being escorted out of Wrigley Field. Fans even threatened his life, so that he had to go into hiding. Watching this show cemented our life long allegiance to the Chicago White Sox.

Athletics has become a lucrative industry where athletes, coaches and owners make millions of dollars annually. Please remember that sports are for entertainment and exercise. Sports should be fun for everyone involved. Parents should instill this idea into their children and never ruin it for them by being unruly fans or overbearing coaches.

Chapter 25: Lifelong Athlete

Staying active has always been an important part of my life. While I was a coach and trainer to my daughter, I was also the captain of

---

[28] Teaching myself the "gainer" off the high dive

a co-ed volleyball team that won the league championship four years in a row. I was also the starting quarterback for a couple of flag football teams and the point guard in a couple of basketball leagues. My flag football team won the championship one year.

I test black belts at a taekwondo school once a year, as their "grand master." The students of this school eagerly look forward to playing with and against me in football after the test. After one "highlight" play that I made in a flag football game, some of my teammates called me "the Asian Sensation."

I enjoyed my taekwondo school's annual picnics, when my students were able to see my athletic skills, aside from martial arts. On one occasion, I teamed with the female members of the Wheaton College Taekwondo Club and challenged the male members to a game of football. I was the quarterback for the girls and designed trick plays. We won, of course!

LIFE LESSON: "Age is just a number." It's never too late to teach "an old dog new tricks." There are numerous examples of people who became "late bloomers" or athletes who competed at a high level well past their "prime" against people less than half their age:

- Ken Griffey Sr. played on the same baseball team with his son, Ken Griffey Jr.
- Gordie Howe played in the NHL at 52 years of age and at one point was the teammate of TWO of his sons
- George Blanda played in the NFL until he was 48
- George Foreman was still a champion boxer at age 45
- President George H. W. Bush parachuted (skydiving) until age 90!

Here are some of my personal examples:

- I learned how to formally dance Latin and Swing in my late 40s.

- I taught myself to perform a "Gainer," a backflip off a diving board while facing forward, also in my late 40s.
- I still play sports against teenagers and people in their 20s. For example, I played basketball against and guarded Jack, the son of a Chicago Bulls' coach, Fred Hoiberg. He was a starting point guard in high school, while his *father*, a former Bulls' shooting guard, was significantly younger than me.
- After my daughter and I beat people in their 20s in beach volleyball when I was in my 50s, they asked her if I was her brother.

I played all these sports and more on a recreational but competitive basis. I sometimes showed up to work with black eyes or swollen lips, from being hit by opponents' elbows or other hard body parts during basketball games. When patients or friends would ask, "What happened?" I would always joke, "You should see the other guy!"

I initially went to the emergency room to receive stitches or to put my finger back in place after a dislocation. Eventually, I performed these minor procedures on myself, and, on more than one occasion, stayed in the game afterwards. I've relocated a dislocated finger too many times to count, in order to keep playing.

I remember watching the movie "Rambo" and thinking that it was cool when he stitched his own laceration on his arm. So, I started doing this. Initially, I sutured myself. I once asked my mom to hold down my bottom lip while I put stitches in it. Now, with the advancement in medicine I am able to use staples or glue.

One sport that I have not played regularly is golf, the exception being my hospital's annual golf outing. Miraculously, I did win a "closest to the pin" contest one year, and the other physicians shook their heads because they knew how seldom I played. Not playing golf on a regular basis is in line with my philosophy of not wanting to be trendy or stereotypical (that "all doctors golf").

Try to stay active for all of your life. Don't use age as an excuse to avoid physical activity. Find physical activities that you enjoy and do them regularly. To avoid boredom, try a different activity everyday and try out new sports, dances, or exercises.

Chapter 26: Marital Kombat

Tragically for my daughter and me, Danielle became unhappy and unsatisfied with our marriage. She asked for a separation from me when Abygale was 10 years old.

I will be the first to admit that it can be very difficult to live with a perfectionist, which I can be. I will also say that when a partner is very organized and *needs* a sense of organization, while the other person cannot provide or go along with this, peace is difficult to achieve. There are some lessons that I learned during marriage and the divorce process, some of which can apply to life in general.

Date your spouse and "keep the spark alive." Your children are of the utmost importance and a gift from God. But, if you value your marriage, have regular date nights or vacations without children. If more people would "court" during marriage, then less marriages would end up in court. Children love to see their parents express their love and devotion to each other.

Feelings aren't everything and they can be very unreliable. Love is not merely a feeling. It also entails commitment, sacrifice and sometimes dishing out discipline (tough love). While people should thoroughly enjoy life and abundantly live every minute of their lives, they should live by principles and not make decisions based on feelings. It is dangerous to base decisions on feelings, as they can vary from one second to the next. I have witnessed people throw away their lives, relationships, or careers because they make rash decisions based on their temporary feelings.

Try to overcome your narcissistic tendencies. Even though society condemns public figures who are self-centered narcissists, people make decisions that are "me first." I believe that society (and marriages) would be improved if it did not follow this pattern, and instead if more people were selfless and self-sacrificing. I do admit that while this may sound undemanding, it is very difficult to do. Advice: "just do it" or at least "try it". You will start feeling better about yourself when you put others' needs before your own. It sounds contradictory, but it works!

Admit when you are wrong, and don't be afraid to say that you are sorry. Do not get in the habit of blaming someone or making illegitimate excuses. Swallow your pride and take ownership of your own actions. On the receiving end, accept sincere apologies; forgive. Don't hold grudges. Don't live with bitterness. Try to live in peace with as many people as possible. Don't worry about those people that do not have the same mindset as you do. "Let go and let God."

*****

The separation of her parents initially hit Abygale very hard, as you can imagine. I remember her saying to me, "I have friends from divorced families, but I never thought it would happen to me!" I do not have divorce among my family members, so I did not think it would happen to me either.

Abygale's academic and athletic progress suffered, at least mildly. She also displayed some physical symptoms ranging from shortness of breath, chest and abdominal pain, to insomnia. I recall singing a lullaby to her over the phone until she fell asleep, after Danielle and Abygale's maternal grandmother were unsuccessful in comforting her and making her fall asleep. I used to regularly sing lullabies to Abygale until she fell asleep when she was growing up.

A few years into the separation, I received a plaque from my daughter for Father's Day that reads "Some people don't believe in HEROES but they haven't met my Dad." I absolutely cherish it and keep it on my desk at work. To this day, my daughter and I remain very close, and she desires to become a physician like her dad.

When Abygale was a junior in high school, she asked me, "Do you plan to retire anytime soon?" I said, "No. Why?" She replied, "Maybe we can work together." Needless to say, this was an incredibly heartwarming moment. Abygale wrote one of her essays for college applications about me as her inspiration to become a physician, and I hope to continue to live up her view of me as a role model.

During the divorce process, I was reassured by female friends who had grown up in broken homes that, "Abygale will become stronger as a result of this." I had my doubts, but these words have turned out to be very prophetic.

Abygale became very self-motivated in high school. She earned straight A's and graduated as her class valedictorian. She earned a *composite* score of 34 on the ACT exam, not merely in the math section like her dad. She was also selected homecoming queen in her senior year, by her peers and faculty. She accomplished all of these things while playing both tennis and volleyball at the same time, fall season, at the varsity level for all four years.

My daughter became a varsity starter in volleyball, starting in her sophomore year. She also became an all-state tennis player for three years, and earned third place (in doubles) in the Illinois State (IHSA) tournament in her junior and senior years. She was named captain of her tennis team in her junior and senior years and a co-captain in volleyball during her senior year.

Abygale also participated in several mission trips to developing countries with her school and church, and completed an internship at my hospital, where she shadowed physicians of various specialties. She has been interviewed for several newspaper articles about her achievements in athletics and academics. Abygale was selected for the IHSA All State Academic team, an honor given only to 26 students each year from all of Illinois. My daughter has experienced the exact high school life that I dreamed of having when I was in high school. I am incredibly proud of her and honored to be her father.

I learned from my marriage and took the time to be there for my daughter so she could have every opportunity to develop into an amazing young woman.

LIFE LESSON: Fatherhood can be an incredibly rewarding and fulfilling role in a man's life. On the other hand, raising a child can be extremely challenging. My advice is simple: LOVE = TIME. Spend quality time and a quantity of time with your children. Guide them and then let them develop into their own young men and women. "Let go and let God."

Chapter 27: Mercy Tragedy

My life has been filled with many more blessings than tragedies. Occasionally, there have been events that suddenly arise that reminds me how life is fleeting. On November 20, 2018, while I was busy treating patients at my clinic, I received several texts

---

[29] My daughter with ER physician Dr. O'Neal

from concerned friends asking if I was OK. I was confused and replied, "Of course. Why do you ask?" Each of them replied that they had heard about a shooting at Mercy Hospital, which is my hospital and employer.

I had been at the hospital that morning, prior to coming to work at my clinic. While finishing seeing my patients, I turned on the news on my computer and the TV. It felt surreal, seeing such violence happening "so close to home."

A gunman shot and killed his ex-fiance, who was an emergency physician at Mercy, and whom my daughter had shadowed for a day in January. The perpetrator then went inside the hospital and randomly shot and killed a pharmaceutical resident and a responding Chicago police officer before he shot and killed himself, after he was wounded by another police officer.

That evening, after finishing work at my clinic, I returned to "the scene of the crime," Mercy Hospital, to soak it all in, since it felt surreal watching it on TV. I talked with some colleagues as well as a responding police officer who was a childhood friend and former taekwondo student at my father's school. Being there made me wonder, had I been there earlier when the shooting was happening, if I could have possibly snuck up on the shooter to subdue him. When tragedies arise, we must remember to not live with regret but find a way to learn from the incident.

That night, I shared the news with my daughter, that the ER doctor that she had shadowed and who had voted for Abygale as high school athlete of the week, was shot and killed. Prior to that day, my daughter had not experienced a tragic death. I thank God that she handled the news gracefully and remained strong, continuing her high school prowess and future career in medicine.

I have already written about this, but I will emphasize it more. Life is short. You never know when it is "your time to go." Say "I love you" to your loved ones. Treasure every minute you have with them. Try to live your life to the fullest everyday.

Chapter 28: Fame Resurrected

From around 1997 until Facebook became popular and commonplace, my fame as a Mortal Kombat 2 character faded into anonymity. I imagined that shows like "Where Are They Now?"

---

[30] Daniel Pesina and me on stage in Argentina

might one day interview the original people who brought the Mortal Kombat characters into pop culture. While this did not happen, Facebook, Google and the popularity of retro video games resurrected Mortal Kombat 2's popularity.

Some of my patients googled my name and found out about my "A.K.A." At their visits some of them have asked, "Why didn't you tell us that you were Shang Tsung in Mortal Kombat 2?" I have answered, "You never asked!" Some patients have subsequently become my fans.

In the summer of 2010, Daniel Pesina and I were invited to attend the grand opening of what would quickly become the biggest arcade in the world, Galloping Ghost Arcade (GGA) in Brookfield, Illinois. The owner, Doc Mack, later told me that I had given him an autographed photo when Mortal Kombat 2 was initially popular.

Throughout the following years I was invited to attend more events at Galloping Ghost, including television interviews,

Mortal Kombat 2 tournaments, and reunions with fellow Mortal Kombat characters, which evolved from "Shang Tsung's Fight Night" to "Kombat Kon". Until these reunions, I had not met all of the people who filmed for Mortal Kombat 3 and later versions of Mortal Kombat. Everyone was glad to get together and share old memories, as well as "bask in the glory" of the old days.

Fans from all over the world (e.g., Puerto Rico, Chile, Belgium, Luxembourg, Malta and Australia) attended these events. Some people wanted to compete in the tournaments, but everyone wanted to meet and mingle with the original Mortal Kombat characters.

Many of these people told me that they have been fans for over 20 years and that I was their childhood "hero." Whenever I hear such statements, I am truly humbled. It has been fun and a great honor for me to meet and get to know such loyal fans. Some fans brought items for me to sign that I had never seen, such as trading cards (some made by fans themselves), action figures (some currently being sold for $300), posters, magazines, and shirts.

 One year, Galloping Ghost Arcade invited the leading Mortal Kombat players from all over the world to compete in Galloping Ghost's tournament, "Shang Tsung's Fight Night." The invitations were autographed by me and were mailed to each person via an elaborate scroll, like in the movie "Mortal Kombat." After the tournament, it was revealed to me by fans that one of the gamers tried to sell his scroll on eBay for $3000. The seller received lots of negative comments for this, and temporarily took it off the market. He eventually sold it for $2500. Fans are also the ones who informed me that I was part of IMDb (Internet Movie Database) and a Mortal Kombat Wiki.

 Some people have asked for my opinion about the Mortal Kombat movie. It is similar to and parallels Bruce Lee's "Enter the Dragon" as I have previously noted. But unlike this movie, I don't consider Mortal Kombat the movie a "classic." In my opinion, it does not even belong in the same class of "classics" as "the Karate Kid," "the Teenage Mutant Ninja Turtles," "Rocky," "The Last Dragon" or even "Bloodsport." The acting was OK; the man who played Shang Tsung (Cary-Hiroyuki Tagawa) was a good actor, but some were so-so.

Some of the martial arts, especially those of the ninjas, were good. Other fight scenes, including those involving Johnny Cage and Shang Tsung would definitely have been better if the original characters (Daniel Pesina and myself) had been involved. Steven Ho, who played Liu Kang's brother Chan, hardly had any fight scenes even though he is a well-established martial artist. Raiden had no fight scenes that involved martial arts. Those who played him were established actors, but professional martial artists should have been used as their doubles. And why does Kano have an Australian accent? Overall, the Mortal Kombat movie was no worse than the movie, "Street Fighter," which I also don't consider a classic.

The above movie review is mainly based on the first Mortal Kombat movie, because I hardly remember the sequel. By the way, I once met Lawrence Kasanoff, who produced the Mortal Kombat movies, when he visited Midway. I don't remember anything specific about him. I do remember Pat Johnson, who was the fight choreographer for the Mortal Kombat movies (as well as the Karate Kid and TMNT movies). He seemed down to earth, both physically (he was shorter than me) and figuratively.

Fans have also asked for my opinion of the Mortal Kombat games that have been released after my participation in Mortal Kombat 2. I am extremely pleased when fans consider me "the original Shang Tsung." I have met John Turk, who played Shang Tsung in Mortal Kombat 3; he is a really nice guy. I have not seen any other Shang Tsung characters in any other Mortal Kombat versions, so I have no opinion.

Because I am a physician as well as a busy dad, I rarely play video games. When I do, it is nearly always Mortal Kombat 2.

I have rarely seen other versions of Mortal Kombat being played. From what I have seen, the graphics are more "gory" or bloody, and the moves are more complicated, but the characters are less realistic. As far as I know, fans do not equate any character with a real person who played that character, in contrast to Mortal Kombat, Mortal Kombat 2 and Mortal Kombat 3.

As a result of the resurrected fame, some of us Mortal Kombat 2 characters were invited to attend comic cons, retro gaming conventions, and other events, both in the United States and overseas. Because I received thousands of friend requests on Facebook, I decided to create a fan page, "Phillip Ahn, M.D./Shang Tsung Mortal Kombat 2."

Most of my fans live outside of the United States, especially in Latin America. Daniel Pesina has been able to attend many of these events that I have mentioned. He has invited me, at the request of event organizers, to attend some of these with him. Work and my daughter have kept me very busy, so I have been able to attend events only when my schedule allowed for travel. The first international events that I attended were in Argentina (Buenos Aires and Cordova) in 2016.

While on stage in Buenos Aires, I felt like a rock star, especially after dancing bachata with one of the fans in attendance who cosplayed Raiden. The fans cheered and chanted my name after this. As I was leaving the stage I gave "low fives" to the audience in the front row next to the stage, and posed for a photo with a couple and their baby. In Cordova, we were on the same stage where the rock band "Whitesnake" had played the previous night. Indeed, I felt like a rock star in Argentina. I was both honored and humbled.

In the summer of 2017, several Mortal Kombat characters and I were invited to attend a gaming expo in Arizona. At that event, we signed autographs for fans, as usual at such events. As a surprising bonus, I was able to meet and dance swing, salsa and bachata with the videogame voice-over actresses: Zelda from

Legend of Zelda, and Sombra and Symmetra from Overwatch. Fun times!

In 2018 Daniel Pesina, Anthony Marquez (who played Kung Lao in Mortal Kombat 2 and Mortal Kombat 3) and I were invited to attend a retro gaming event in Norway. I signed autographs for fans but also hung out with some other gaming celebrities, like Charles Martinet, the voice actor for the Mario brothers. While in Norway, we were invited to march in their Independence Day parade.

In March 2019, seven of us Mortal Kombat and Mortal Kombat 2 characters were invited to sign autographs, take photographs, as well as give a Q and A panel at Chicago Comic and Entertainment Expo (C2E2). During this weekend, I also met the main characters from one of my favorite movies about which I have made references in this book, the "Karate Kid."

As a bonus, I reunited with Sombra from Overwatch and met Mercy from the same game at C2E2. I took them and two of their girlfriends out to dance salsa and bachata. Yes, four women and me; don't be jealous. I had already danced with Sombra, so she knew what to expect, but the rest were very impressed at how well I can dance and lead those who don't know how to dance. Even at conventions, I found time to stay active, meet people and pursue my interests.

The resurrection of my fame as Shang Tsung in Mortal Kombat 2 has brought me incredibly rewarding and fun opportunities. I look forward to continuing to meet interesting people, both fans and celebrities, in the United States and throughout the world.

Chapter 29: Dance Fever

As previously mentioned, my ex-wife Danielle asked for a separation, which eventually ended in divorce after nearly five and a half years. During my separation period before my divorce, I was introduced to the world of dance.

---

[31] Dancing Bachata with a Raiden cosplayer on stage in Argentina

Prior to the separation, I had considered myself a pretty good dancer, even having participated in a breakdance routine in a college talent show with three other students. My strongest move was the "upside down moonwalk" on my head. If break dancing didn't first become popular when I was studying pre-medicine, I would definitely have practiced more, so that I could have become proficient at the more athletic acrobatic moves, like the "helicopter" and "flares".

Even though I grew up shy, I eventually "broke out of my shell" and even became the first to "start the party" by encouraging the dancing at weddings and similar events. I remember that one night I was watching a rerun of "Saturday Night Fever" on TV. I memorized the line dance from the movie. I told myself, "The next wedding I attend, I'm going to lead everyone in this dance." I have indeed done this, at weddings and other parties.

I was invited on some occasions to go out dancing salsa and other Latin dances during my marriage, by my office staff members, who have all been Latinas. I declined their invitations while I was married. Shortly after separating from Danielle, I was again invited to a salsa party by one of my former staff members. This time I did attend the event.

Before attending this event, I considered myself a good dancer who could pick up any dance. Watching the dancers, I realized that salsa is distinct and creatively challenging. The people at this party appeared like professional dancers to me. I even said to myself, "Some of these people are old white folks. How come they know how to salsa and I don't? What's wrong with this picture?"

In general, I hate the feeling of not being good at something that I choose to do. It took nearly three months to swallow my pride, but I eventually began taking salsa lessons and slowly (some say quickly) became a proficient Latin dancer.

Less than one year into starting salsa lessons, I was invited to be a guest instructor for the Latin Dance Club at my alma mater,

Wheaton College. The college did not even allow social dancing when I was a student there! My family had attended Wheaton's inaugural social dance when my daughter was two and a half years old.

These days, other dancers ask if I am an instructor or if I compete, to which I reply, "No." I am simply a "social dancer." I do tell beginner salsa dancers, that they should try to follow these simple principles when they dance salsa, and these all begin with the letter "S":

1) "Slow" – Beginners tend to dance faster than their leader and or the song rhythm. This is either because they are nervous or because the song seems fast, when in reality it is not, if you break the rhythm down.

2) "Small" – You can tell an inexperienced dancer when you see him or her taking big steps, sometimes resulting in stepping on other dancers or throwing off their rhythm count.

3) "Smooth" – Don't be rough or bouncy when you take your steps or lead your partner. Also, do not make big and rough swinging motions with your arms.

4) "Soft" – Followers compliment me on my soft (and smooth) lead. The opposite of soft, in dance, would be "stiff," which beginners often are, because they are nervous. Some followers are extremely soft and have "spaghetti arms." Both of these scenarios make it difficult and unpleasant to dance with them, especially because they can throw off the rhythm count. Try to find the right "balance".

5) "Spot" – When you learn to surf, they instruct you not to look at the water, but find a spot and look straight ahead. As a dancer, don't look at your feet. Look straight ahead. This will help you with balance and help you avoid getting dizzy. Keeping your head up also makes you look confident.

Dancing has many benefits:

- It is a good form of exercise for both your body and your brain.
- It meets social needs. You don't even have to make plans or "dates" because there is usually a dance event going on.
- It helps keep you young. It is unique in that people of all ages and races can dance with each other.
- It can fix your posture. You are taught to keep your back straight when you dance. If you apply this habit on a daily basis, you will gain confidence, which in turn will elevate your mood and decrease anxiety and depression.

Taking salsa lessons has allowed me to pick up and even become good or proficient at other social dances, especially swing and its variations. As mentioned earlier, I danced bachata onstage in Buenos Aires with a Raiden cosplayer, and I also danced "hustle" (Cuarteto in Argentina) with a popular Anime singer in Cordova. My later participation in the dance world is why I mentioned that a dance as my "Friendship" in Mortal Kombat 2 would have been more fitting for me than for Liu Kang.

Because of dance, I was able to find a healthy way to deal with a stressful period in my life. By finding a healthy social activity, I made many new friends and began to "master" a new skill. I look forward to what opportunities dancing may bring in my future, whether it's competing on television or meeting interesting personalities.

As I continue to improve as a social dancer, I will strive to be a better martial artist, medical doctor, father, and friend. Living a fulfilled life does not only mean being "good at" your job, relationships, or hobbies. You also need to be willing to learn new skills. If you desire to "thrive, not just survive," take the time to nurture all aspects of your life.

Author's Note

I thank God every single day for the incredibly blessed life that He has allowed me to live. In spite of some tragedies, mistakes and tough lessons, my journey has been one full of adventure, joy, and people who love and support me.

I love serving my patients, both in Chicago and in developing countries. I love traveling; I still have many places to visit on my "buckct list." I love being a father and having an incredible relationship with my daughter. I love and appreciate all of my fans, friends and family.

I look forward to improving every aspect of my life, every day. In the years to come look for me to be a part of martial arts related projects, video games, and of course meeting more fans at Mortal Kombat 2 events all over the world.

I have more stories, Mortal Kombat 2 related and otherwise. Maybe I can share these stories in the sequel "Mortal Doctor 2"!

Favorite Quotes

Besides the quotes that I have already written throughout this book, here are some quotes that have inspired me and that I hope will have a similar effect on my readers:

- "When I stand before God at the end of my life, I would hope that I would not have a single bit of talent left, and could say, 'I used everything you gave me'."

    ~Erma Bombeck

- "What good is it for a man to gain the whole world but lose his soul?" *~Matthew 16:26*

- "Have nothing to do with godless myths and old wives tales; rather, train yourself to be godly." *~1 Timothy 4:7*

- "I have fought the good fight, I have finished the race, I have kept the faith." *~2 Timothy 4:7*

- "Do not pray for an easy life; pray for the strength to endure a difficult one." ~*Bruce Lee*
- "You can't be common because the common man goes nowhere" ~*Herb Brooks*, coach of the United States "Miracle on Ice" hockey team.
- "To be unstoppable you have to be unpredictable" ~*Kobe Bryant*
- "Be afraid of the calmest person in the room." ~*Bruce Lee*
- "Veni, vidi, vici" (I came, I saw, I conquered.") ~*Julius Caesar*
- "Cogito Ergo Sum" ("I think, therefore I am.") ~René Descartes
- "An unexamined life is not worth living." ~*Socrates*
- "Only boring people get bored." ~*Ruth Burke*
- "Bring it!" "It's already been brung!" ~*Phillip Ahn*
- "Let's make like a fetus and head out." ~*unknown*
- "Let's make like a cookie and 가자." ~*Phillip Ahn*

Favorite Yogi Berra Quotes

- "Baseball is 90 percent physical; the other half is mental."

- "Always go to other people's funerals, or they won't go to yours."

- "What time is it?" "You mean right now?"

- "It gets late early out there."

- "Nobody goes there anymore. It's too crowded."

- "It's difficult to make predictions, especially about the future."

- "When you get to a fork in the road, take it."

Favorite Jokes

Disclaimer: Humor is often found through the miscommunication and differences between people. Almost none of these jokes are of my own creation and have been told to me throughout my life.

Q. What do people do if they are agnostic and dyslexic, and have insomnia?"

A. *They stay up all night, wondering if there really is a dog."*

Q. What do you call a short fortune teller on the run from the law?

A. *A small medium at large.*

Q. Why did the football coach go to the bank?

A. *To get his Quarterback!*

Q. Why did the defensive coordinator go to the bank?

A. *To get his Nickelback!*

Q. If you are American before you enter the bathroom and after you exit the bathroom, what are you when you are in the bathroom?

A. *European (You're peein')*

Q. What if you have to use the bathroom very badly?

A. *You're Russian (Rushin')*

Q. And when you're done?

A. *You're Finnish (Finished)*

Q. What is Bruce Lee's favorite drink?

A. *Water (say it like he would in his movies – "wah-tah")!*

Q. What is Bruce Lee's favorite fast food?

A. *Whopper ("wah-pah")!*

Q. What is Bruce Lee's favorite hotel?

A. *Hyatt!*

Q. Two nuns snuck in a bottle of liquor into a baseball game and eventually became drunk. At that point, what inning was it and how many people were on base?

A. It was the bottom of the fifth and the bags were loaded!

Sylvester Stallone, Bruce Willis and Arnold Schwarzenegger enrolled in music appreciation class. One day the instructor told them, "Today we are going to pretend that we are classical composers." Stallone spoke up and said, "I'll be Mozart." Willis said, "I'll be Beethoven." They looked at Arnold, who turned to them and said, "I'll be Bach."

I was going to tell a joke about Sodium, but then I thought, "Na", people won't understand!

I was going to tell a joke about Nitric Oxide, but then I thought, "NO", people won't understand!

I was going to tell a joke about Nitrous Oxide, but I thought too many people would die laughing!

Vocabulary for First Year Medical Students

Artery	The study of paintings
Bacteria	Back door of cafeteria
Barium	What doctors do when a patient dies
Bowel	A letter A,E,I,O, or U
Cesarean section	A neighborhood in Rome
Cat scan	Searching for kitty
Cauterize	Made eye contact with her
Colic	A sheep dog
Coma	A punctuation mark
D & C	Where Washington is
Dilate	To live long
Enema	Not a friend
Fester	Quicker
Fibula	A small lie
Genital	Not a Jew
G.I. series	A soldier ballgame
Hangnail	Coat hook
Impotent	Distinguished, well known

Labor pain	Getting hurt at work
Medical staff	A doctor's cane
Morbid	A higher offer
Nitrates	Cheaper than day rates
Node	Was aware of
Outpatient	A person who has fainted
Pap-smear	A fatherhood test
Pelvis	A cousin to Elvis
Post-operative	Letter carrier
Recovery room	Place to do upholstery
Rectum	Dang near killed 'em
Secretion	Hiding something
Seizure	Roman emperor
Tablet	A small table
Terminal illness	Getting sick at the airport
Tumor	More than one
Urine	Opposite of "you're out"
Varicose	Nearby
Vein	Conceited

True stories, from a daily desk calendar I received for Christmas:

A medical student was interviewing a female patient during his OB Gyn rotation: Q. "When was your last menstrual period?"

A. *"I be havin' it right now."*

Q. "What type of flow do you have?"

A. *"Linoleum!"*

A visiting French gynecologist with limited English skills was using a checklist to interview his patients, when an older female came in for her appointment. In his thick French accent he asked her: "Do you have herpes?" She answered, "Yes." He was a bit startled, so he asked her again, "You have herpes?" She answered, "Actually, it's a full wig!"

A Filipino ER nurse came out of a patient's room frantically yelling "Chicken Nut Bread." Everyone was confused until the ER attending treated the patient and reassured everyone that "She can breathe now."

A nurse in the ER asked a female patient, "Are you sexually active?" The patient replied, "No." The nurse performed a pregnancy test anyway, and it came back positive. She went back to the patient, showed her the results of the test, and said, "I thought you said that you are not sexually active!" The patient answered, "I'm not; I just lay there!"

A labor and delivery nurse asked a new mom, "What are you going to name your baby?" The patient answered, "I don't have to; the doctor already named her." The nurse was puzzled and asked the patient, "What do you mean?" She replied, "Look in the chart. He named her 'Fe-ma-lie.'" The nurse looked in the chart and noticed that the chart read, "Baby female!"

A woman in labor was rushed to the nearest hospital. The obstetrician on call introduced himself, "I'm Dr. Smith, at your cervix." Without missing a beat, the patient replied, "Dilated to meet you!

Appendix

For more photos, articles and exclusive content, visit:

www.mortaldoctor.com

Connect with Phillip Ahn, M.D. on:

Facebook: Shang Tsung MK2 **fb.me/shangtsungmk2/**

Instagram: https://www.instagram.com/ahn.phillip/

Photo credits: Marisela Guerra

(cover photo and Parenthood photo #2)